Mathamazement

Also by Ronn Yablun:

How to Develop Your Child's Gifts and Talents in Math

Mathamazement

Ronn Yablun

LOWELL HOUSE
Los Angeles

CONTEMPORARY BOOKS
Chicago

Library of Congress Cataloging-in-Publication Data

Yablun, Ronn.
    Mathamazement / by Ronn Yablun.
        p.   cm.
    ISBN 1-56565-454-4
    1. Mathematics—Study and teaching (Elementary)   I. Title.
QA135.5.Y34   1996
510—dc20   96-8074
                                                                                              CIP

Requests for such permissions should be addressed to:

    Lowell House
    2029 Century Park East, Suite 3290
    Los Angeles, CA 90067

Lowell House books can be purchased at special discounts when ordered in
bulk for premiums and special sales. Contact Department JH at the address
above.

Publisher: Jack Artenstein
General Manager, Lowell House Adult: Bud Sperry
Managing Editor: Maria Magallanes
Text design: Susan H. Hartman

Manufactured in the United States of America

10   9   8   7   6   5   4   3   2   1

Acknowledgments

Special thanks to Gloria Patterson for her ears; Sharon Wheeler for her invaluable advice; John Anderson and Carol Lidgen, my mentors; Michael Warnecke for always giving me "time off"; Steve Richardson for his input; Bud Sperry for always pushing me; Beth Matustik for always being there; and to all my students past and present for teaching more than I could ever teach them.

This book is lovingly dedicated to my mother and father.

Contents

Introduction

When I graduated from college in 1972, I had every intention of diving into a teaching job—in art, not math. My original undergraduate major was art education. I had completed my student teaching at the high school level in art and was fully prepared to proceed in that direction. However, not only were there no art teaching positions available, there were few teaching jobs of any kind to be had anywhere. I resigned myself to working other jobs until such time when a teaching job would present itself to me. Patience did pay off, but in a most unusual way.

The first teaching job came five years later, in 1977, when I was offered a position at a private junior and senior high school. During an interview, I was asked if I could teach math. I responded, "Certainly." Now, I hadn't seen a math book since my junior year in high school (that was in 1967!), and here I was to face five classes of basic math, algebra, and geometry. I found it less difficult to teach these classes than I had originally expected. Of course, I was lucky math came easy to me. I found that keeping one chapter ahead of my students gave me the necessary distance to stay on top of the subjects and on top of students' questions.

Sometimes one may pause to think how past events contribute to one's present sense of purpose. Within six months I realized that teaching math was to be my life's work. I went back to school, picked up the math classes I needed for my California teacher's credential, and the rest, as the saying goes, is history (actually in my case, the rest is math).

After sixteen years in the classroom, I am just as excited about teaching this subject as I was when I started. While I recognize how my position carries an incredible responsibility to my students, I know that it also allows me to affect lives daily. This in itself is truly an awesome thought!

For the past thirteen years, I have taught junior high school classes. Most people, upon hearing that, quickly offer their condolences! I, on the other hand, know what I and my students would be missing if I were elsewhere.

Coincidentally, also thirteen years ago, I opened MATHAMAZEMENT—a learning center and now also the title of this book—to assist students having difficulty in math. I knew there existed a need in our community for solid, professional assistance in math for kids of all ages. My initial intentions were to reach as many kids as possible and not to be limited only to those who passed through my classroom doors. The results suggest that my plan was right on target.

Occasionally I reflect again upon the circumstances surrounding my math beginnings and wonder where I would be and what I would be doing if things hadn't happened exactly the way they did. Not a day goes by that I don't count my blessings for being able to do exactly what I love doing most. I also feel fortunate in that I have often been told that I have a way of explaining things in terms that people understand. To me, the gift in math is not necessarily the mathematical knowledge, but the ability to translate that knowledge into basic terms people understand. I have always believed that a math teacher, no matter how brilliant a mathematician, was worth his salt only if he could translate his knowledge into basic, understandable skills.

This brings me to the subject of this book. Math, as most of us know it today, is largely comprised of numbers that we use to solve problems. Did you ever stop to think, "Whoever thought about number problems and started the math ball rolling?" Depending on whom you ask, you're likely to get a variety of answers. Yet, technologically, the advancements that math has achieved since its very humble beginnings might dazzle anyone. From stone slabs to computers, from the advent of the wheel to the exploration of space, math is the heart and soul of practically every invention and advancement we have heard of or witnessed to date. Most people don't think of math in terms of computers and space travel, yet they are integral parts of the program. Math serves as the foundation for so many advancements. Think about computers, CDs, aviation, cellular phones, fax machines—math is largely responsible for all these and more. I could go on and on, but now I'd like to get to the real purpose of this book.

It is my desire and my intention to make this math experience both fun and easy at the same time. I, myself, have encountered situations where someone is trying to explain something to me and I don't have a clue as to what they are talking about. I know how frustrating it is to be on the receiving end of a cloudy explanation. I also know that when I am receiving a clear and precise explanation, I am more receptive to the presenter and more attentive to what is going on . . . and a lot more at ease with the situation. It is my intention, hopefully, to be more representative of the latter.

With this book I hope to show you that math can be made easy, it can be challenging, and, most importantly, it can be fun. When I speak to people about math, their reactions are usually one of the following: Either it was fairly easy for them during their school years, or it was a horrific experience they wished no one would ever have to go through. Unfortunately, most of the people I have spoken with immediately tell me of their personal nightmares with math. By comparison, I was definitely one of the luckier ones, and I firmly believe that I have my teachers to thank for this. Two in particular come to mind: Miss Carol Lidgen and Mr. John Anderson, both at Maine East High School in Park Ridge, Illinois, who taught me algebra and geometry, respectively. They are the ones who made math easy and fun for me. They are the ones who explained everything to me in a way that I understood and whose patience became a model for me. I have no doubt that they were especially responsible for my successes with math.

It is my intention here to carry on this legacy of good teaching and do what it is that everyone tells me I do best: "Explain it." I hope that by the time you finish this book you will feel enlightened and, even more, enthralled by the magic of numbers. I have learned through my own experiences with math that numbers have the most phenomenal characteristics. The tricks you can do with them and the fun you can have with them truly make numbers magical! Unlike all other languages, math is the only one I know of that has so many different approaches and directions— seemingly endless possibilities.

Although we are usually unaware of it in our everyday lives, math is forever playing a role. It definitely plays a larger role for some than for others, but if you really thought about how much math you deal with daily, you would probably be very surprised. Try for one entire day to keep track of the math skills you use as you use them. Then you might see that I'm telling you the truth about the impact math has on your life!

It is also my intention to make math easier for you. Hopefully, the tricks and shortcuts I demonstrate will help you move faster and with more accuracy in the math that you encounter on a daily basis. The puzzles and games I present will entertain, challenge, and stimulate you. This book could make a significant change in the way you perceive math as it directly relates to you. Most importantly, I hope you have fun with it and always remember that math is "just a bunch of numbers!" And for some people, this is a good thing.

Whole Numbers

My students often ask me why we have to learn math and who was responsible for "inventing" it. I usually tell them that some ancient Greeks—former friends of mine, no doubt—had nothing better to do with their time since they didn't have CD players and computers to tinker with. You might be amazed that these students have to stop and consider how these things might be true. I then explain to them how money evolved from basic bartering for services and products, leading to the evolution of modern currency systems, for which they begin to recognize a "real" use for math. They certainly keep me in check when it comes to dealing with math skills and their unique perception of math as a totally disjointed fragment of reality. "What am I going to use this for in life?" they ask, or "Why do we have to learn this?" You would be very surprised to find that they haven't a clue as to the many uses of this most practical science. Whole numbers have unique characteristics. They are certainly worth exploring in that you begin to see the many practical uses for numbers.

It makes a great deal of sense to explore whole numbers first since they form the basic foundation for math at almost every level of complexity. Every other level of math branches out from this, the most fundamental of all levels, whose applications reach beyond the imagination.

Fractions, decimals, percents, and even concepts of algebra and geometry utilize the many basic characteristics of whole numbers. Once we have arrived at these other levels of math, you will begin to see exactly how all the pieces of this large puzzle fit together.

But before we launch into even the most basic of operations with whole numbers and the shortcuts and tricks you can use to solve these basic problems, it's helpful first to explore patterns of numbers. Patterns help us to understand the basic characteristics of numbers and how they interact with each other, the effects they have on each other, and the unique relationships they share with each other. When we understand the mechanics of whole numbers and their characteristic patterns, we can also begin to understand relationships that different numbers share with each other.

Patterns

Sequences (or patterns) can range from the very basic to the very complex. Exploring patterns in numbers often helps us understand the mechanics of numbers. How numbers relate to each other, as basic as it may sound, often helps us begin to see relationships in numbers. Number families emerge. We often use these most basic relationships when we perform simple mathematical operations.

For example, knowing that the difference between even whole numbers is two is helpful in addition. When we add two even whole numbers, we know we will get another even whole number as an answer. This is only one example of how the basic knowledge of patterns can be useful.

The most basic sequences, or patterns, involve nothing more than repeatedly adding or subtracting a select whole number. Other sequences involve fractions, decimals, and even algebraic or geometric concepts that require more knowledge and expertise to solve. I've given you several sequences to explore. First, you will need to determine how the first term leads to the second term, then how the second term leads to the third term, and so on. See if you can recognize the consistent pattern that describes the changes from one number to the next. With this approach in mind, try to find the next three terms in each sequence. To check yourself, see the answers in the back of the book.

❶ 1, 2, 4, 7, ___, ___, ___

❷ 100, 99, 97, 94, 90, ___, ___, ___

❸ 0, 1, 4, 9, 16, ___, ___, ___

❹ 5, 105, 195, 275, ___, ___, ___

❺ 2, 7, 17, 37, ___, ___, ___

❻ 1, 8, 27, 64, ___, ___, ___

❼ –6, –3, 0, ___, ___, ___

❽ –2, 4, –8, ___, ___, ___

❾ 132, 64, 32, ___, ___, ___

❿ 1, 2, 4, 5, 10, ___, ___, ___

Addition

Often we are faced with a situation where we need to quickly add numbers to arrive at a sum. In such situations, you may not find a calculator (who can when you need one?) so a quick, efficient way to add mentally can save time and frustration. One method involves regrouping by tens to quicken the process of adding whole numbers. Take a look at the problem below:

$$\begin{array}{r} 36 \\ + \ 24 \\ \hline \end{array}$$

Notice that the four and the six on the right add up to ten. Grouping by tens is one way to add quickly. Seeing that the right column (that is, the units column) adds to ten, you simply add one to the sum of the left column. Therefore, the answer is 60.

Take a look at this next problem and see if you can quickly give the sum:

$$\begin{array}{r} 48 \\ + \ 32 \\ \hline \end{array}$$

Again, in the right column we have a sum of ten. Therefore, the answer is one more in the tens column than the sum of 4 and 3. That is, the answer is 80. Now try these; speed is the key.

❶ $\begin{array}{r} 42 \\ + \ 38 \\ \hline \end{array}$

❷   55
    + 75
    ———

❸   61
    + 29
    ———

❹   14
    + 46
    ———

Now let's take this one step further. Let's say that the sum of the digits in the right column exceeds 10. We know from past experiences that we always carry the tens digit to the next column left. Keep this in mind while I explain this next example:

        39
    + 47
    ———

Looking at this problem, I know the answer is 86. Why? Notice that the sum of the digits in the units column exceeds 10. Also, since this column has only two digits, its sum must be less than 20, so the most we can possibly carry is one. Carrying the one makes the sum of the tens column eight. And since the sum of the units column exceeds 10 by 6, I need only write down the 6 in the units column. I already carried the one. A rule of thumb to keep in mind: The largest value you will ever have to carry will be one less than the number of digits in the column.

To test your speed, see how quickly you can add these pairs of numbers:

❺   48
   + 28
   ——————

❻   36
   + 67
   ——————

❼   58
   + 19
   ——————

❽   75
   + 26
   ——————

Now, let's try to adapt this same idea to numbers that are slightly larger. For example, let's deal with a sum of three-digit numbers:

     748
   + 237
   ——————

From our previous discussions, we know that the largest value we will have to carry anywhere in this problem is one. Notice in the units column the sum exceeds 10 by 5, yet in the tens column the sum is less than 10. We will have to carry to the tens column but not to the hundreds column, so by looking at the problem we know that the answer is 985. Knowing these little tricks and being alert will definitely help speed up the process and improve your accuracy. Now try several problems keeping in mind the following:

- Carrying is only necessary if the sum within a column is 10 or greater.

- The greatest value you will ever have to carry is one less than the number of digits in the column.

Now try these:

❾   **357**
   + 229

❿   **629**
   + 157

⓫   **901**
   + 379

⓬   **824**
   + 466

Grouping by tens is probably one of the easiest ways to add. It makes a lot of sense since carrying will occur every time a column reaches a sum of 10. Mentally pairing numbers whose sum is 10 can hasten the process. Take a look at the problem below:

```
  12,495
  18,653
  27,817
+ 43,255
```

Using this pairing process, you still add from right to left as you would using pencil and paper. Notice the units column, where you can pair the two fives and then the three and the seven to get two tens, or 20. It is *not* absolutely necessary to add from top to bottom to arrive at an accurate sum. In the tens column, you can pair the two fives and then the one and the nine to again get two tens, or 20, but don't forget the two carried over from the units column. By this point, you should be able to see the pairings of numbers in the hundreds column—the four with the six, and the eight with the two—again taking into consideration the value carried from the previous column. Finish the problem by continuing the same strategy. When complete, your answer should read 102,220.

Now try this technique on these problems and check your answers in the answer key when finished. Speed and accuracy both count!

⑬   14,357
      26,583
      51,755
      19,525

⑭   26,809
      77,221
      14,388
      53,702

ⓖ   456,202
    114,775
    299,808
    551,335

Now, using this same idea, try to add the following, with the understanding that not all the columns will have digits that pair up by tens. Just remember to carry as needed.

ⓖ   44,298
     26,424
     25,886
     33,835

ⓗ   62,099
     22,519
     11,551
     44,776

ⓘ   258,633
    392,370
    455,066
    185,131

Now, for those who really like a challenge, try the following sums. Use a timer and allow yourself only one minute. See if you can now accomplish the task of adding columns *without* using a calculator.

⑲   27,645
      44,365
      53,777
      34,222
      12,212

⑳   48,699
      19,410
      51,333
      62,351
      78,427

㉑   177,381
      269,622
      555,107
      335,733
      191,377

Subtraction

How do we subtract without a calculator? When regrouping (more commonly known as "borrowing") is involved, most people tend to borrow one column at a time. I have found it easiest to borrow all the way across immediately to quicken the process and save myself both the aggravation and the confusion. Let me demonstrate:

$$27,600$$
$$- 15,323$$

In this problem, you might attempt to borrow one column at a time. I recommend the following: Borrow 1 from 600. (Unfortunately, this technique works *only* with zeros.) This leaves you 599, correct? Use the borrowed 1 in the last column to give you 10 and change the other columns so that the problem now looks like this:

```
  27,59  10
- 15,32   3
 ───────────
  12,27   7
```

Subtracting is now a breeze! Just for practice, try the following and see if it isn't easier this way. I'm sure you will find it is.

❶   27,000
      − 11,293
     ─────────

❷   450,000
      − 143,771
     ─────────

❸   6,880,000
     − 2,366,927
     ─────────

Multiplication

Another of the most basic skills is multiplication. To master this skill, it is important to understand that multiplication is nothing more than repeated addition—that is, an avenue for adding numbers faster. For example, if we multiply 2 times 3, isn't that the same as adding two threes? Either way, the result is 6. Look at the problem again and see if this makes sense.

Now try this one: 12 times 4. Isn't this the same as counting by twelves (or adding 12) four times? Either way, the result is 48.

This basic understanding of the concept of multiplication should make the work much easier. Just for the sake of practice, try writing each of the following multiplication problems as an addition problem before you solve it. This should help you see the strategy we are using here. I've taken the liberty of doing the first problem for you:

❶ 11 × 7
11 + 11 + 11 + 11 + 11 + 11 + 11 = 77
or count by elevens: 11, 22, 33, 44, 55, 66, <u>77</u>
the seventh number is your answer!

❷ 10 × 6

❸ 15 × 5

❹ 12 × 6

❺ 11 × 8

Now try this same idea with larger numbers and see if this simplifies the multiplication process:

❻ 25 × 4

❼ 30 × 3

❽ 50 × 5

❾ 22 × 6

Please keep this "counting" idea in mind as we progress through multiplication so that you remain aware that multiplication is really nothing more than repeated addition.

There are several basic tricks to multiplication that should make the process more of a simple mental exercise. The first trick involves multiplying numbers that end with one or more zeros. Very simply, you multiply all the digits excluding the zeros and then add on to your answer the total number of zeros that were in the original problem. For example:

$$\begin{array}{r} 500 \\ \times\ 30 \\ \hline \end{array}$$

First multiply 5 by 3 to get the result, 15. Then add three zeros to your answer since there are a total of three zeros in the multiplication problem (two zeros in the top row and one zero in the bottom row). The final answer is 15,000. Please note that this procedure does not apply for zeros that are in the middle of either number. They must be at the end of the number. Now try these:

⑩ $\begin{array}{r} 800 \\ \times\ 40 \\ \hline \end{array}$

⑪ $\begin{array}{r} 700 \\ \times\ 80 \\ \hline \end{array}$

⑫ $\begin{array}{r} 600 \\ \times\ 400 \\ \hline \end{array}$

Well, how did you do? If this was *no* problem for you, try this next set. The only difference here is that the numbers are larger. Just keep in mind that the same rule applies.

⑬   8,000
    × 600
    ‾‾‾‾‾‾

⑭   12,000
    ×   400
    ‾‾‾‾‾‾

⑮   15,000
    ×   500
    ‾‾‾‾‾‾

⑯   25,000
    × 3,000
    ‾‾‾‾‾‾

Recall once again that multiplication is nothing more than "repeated addition—short and quick." Now take a look at this simple multiplication problem:

$$\begin{array}{r} 48 \\ \times\ 36 \\ \hline \end{array}$$

Notice that 36 is the same as 30 + 6. So we may consider this problem to be the same as:

$$\begin{array}{r} 48 \\ \times\ 30 \\ \hline 1440 \end{array} \quad + \quad \begin{array}{r} 48 \\ \times\ 6 \\ \hline 288 \end{array} \quad = \quad 1728$$

Take a look at another example:

```
     53
 ×  27
 _____
```

Notice here that 27 is the same as 20 + 7.

```
     53              53
 ×  20          ×   7
 _____         _____
  1060     +     371     =     1431
```

Now that you have a better understanding of this procedure, how about trying a few problems on your own? Do as much of each problem in your head as you can.

⑰   **28**
  × 14

⑱   **56**
  × 35

⑲   **347**
  × 72

⑳   **519**
  × 86

This technique also works with three- and four-digit numbers. See if you can use this same process to solve the following problems. They are tougher and will require a little more patience, but they will work out.

㉑   **427**
  × 516

㉒   566
     × 238
     ─────

㉓   4,621
     × 946
     ─────

㉔   3,809
     × 5,721
     ──────

Division

Division is the one basic math skill for which I strongly recommend the use of a calculator whenever possible.
Because it is tedious to do by hand, division can be the
most frustrating of the basic operations. However, should
you be without a calculator and need solutions, here is the
easiest way to perform division without spending an hour
on any single problem.

If you have a two-digit divisor (the number outside the
division symbol), divide the first digit of that divisor into the
first two digits of the dividend (the number inside). Likewise if you have a three-digit divisor. Here's an example:

$$456 \overline{)137,855}$$

Instead of trying to divide 456 into 1378, divide 4 into 13.
Since you know that 4 times 3 is 12, the most likely first
digit in your answer is 3. Then you multiply 3 by 456,
which is 1368. Place a 3 in the quotient (your answer)

above the 8, place 1368 under 1378 in the dividend, then subtract and proceed as usual. This process should assist you in getting through the problem a little more rapidly. However, I again strongly encourage you to use a calculator whenever possible.

In regards to a calculator, should you divide using a calculator and have a desire to know the exact remainder, there is a trick to figuring that out. It is important to recognize that your calculator will not give you a whole number remainder when you divide. Instead, it will carry out the division into decimal places until the remainder is zero or until there is no room left in the display of the calculator. There is a trick for obtaining the simple remainder.

Suppose we had 4357 items that needed to be packaged into boxes of 12. Dividing 4357 by 12 would tell us how many boxes we would completely fill. Using a calculator, the display would read 363.0833333. This tells us that we would fill 363 boxes. Let's suppose that we also wanted to know how many items would be left after the packaging process. To figure this out you would multiply 363 (the whole number part of the answer in the calculator display) by your original divisor, which in this case is 12. The net result is 4356. Subtract this amount from your original dividend, which in this case is 4357, to get the remainder, 1. Therefore, you now know that you would have exactly one item left after you had packaged the rest into boxes of 12!

Whole Number Puzzles

Whole numbers can be combined in different ways to provide a variety of answers. Those answers are completely dependent on what we do with the numbers in the first place. For example:

Can you arrange four ones to get 4 as an answer?
1 + 1 + 1 + 1 = 4

Can you arrange four ones to get 22 as an answer?
11 + 11 = 22

Can you arrange four ones to get 11 as an answer?
11 − 1 + 1 = 11

Now that you see that numbers can be grouped, arranged, and manipulated to yield a variety of answers, see if you can solve the following:

❶ Can you arrange four ones to get 12?

❷ Can you arrange four twos to get 10?

❸ Can you arrange four threes to get 111?

❹ Can you arrange four fours to get 8?

❺ Can you arrange four fives to get 80?

❻ Can you arrange four sixes to get 17?

❼ Can you arrange five sevens to get 49?

❽ Can you arrange four eights to get 1?

❾ Can you arrange four nines to get 10?

You can check against the solutions in the back of the book to see if you arrived at the same arrangements of numbers. Note that more than one arrangement may be correct.

Now that you have the general idea of how the number puzzles work, try this next set. What you need to do is to insert the correct mathematical symbols between the twos and threes to make each sentence true. You may use plus, minus, times, and divide, as well as parentheses and brackets.

2	2	2	2	=	0
2	2	2	2	=	1
2	2	2	2	=	2
2	2	2	2	=	3
2	2	2	2	=	4
2	2	2	2	=	5
2	2	2	2	=	6
2	2	2	2	=	10
2	2	2	2	=	12

3	3	3	3	=	1
3	3	3	3	=	3
3	3	3	3	=	4
3	3	3	3	=	5
3	3	3	3	=	6
3	3	3	3	=	7
3	3	3	3	=	8
3	3	3	3	=	9
3	3	3	3	=	10

Before we move on to the next topic, I wanted to present you with a whole number puzzle. The directions are self-explanatory. If you are up to the challenge, I think you will truly enjoy this one.

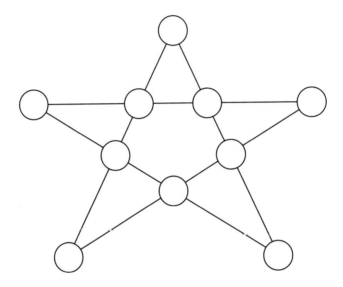

In the star-shaped diagram, there are five rows of circles.
Use the numbers 1, 2, 3, 4, 5, 6, 7, 8, 9, 10, 12
to fill in the circles so that each row has the same sum.
Note that each row contains exactly four circles and each number
should appear exactly once in the diagram.

At this point, I'd like to provide you with a quick review of strategies we explored in this chapter. I hope you will find this "cheat sheet" useful.

CHAPTER CHEAT SHEET

Addition:	Group by tens.
Subtraction:	Borrow all the way across.
Multiplication:	Bring down zeros. Multiply separately by 10's and by 1's, then combine.
Division:	Divide the first digit in the divisor into the first two digits in the dividend.

To bring this section to a close, I would like to restate that whole numbers have many characteristics that lead to easy manipulation. We have spent time discussing short-cuts and strategies that simplify operations with whole numbers. It is my intent to do the same with decimals and fractions in the next chapter. Read on!

Decimals
and Fractions

Decimals and fractions are so closely related that I would be remiss if I were to separate them. Sometimes, it is easier to give an answer as a fraction and sometimes it is easier to give an answer as a decimal. It largely depends on the type of problem. For example, if you are working a fraction problem, it makes sense to give your answer as a fraction. The same holds true for decimals. Yet sometimes it is difficult to separate the two.

It is important to understand that decimals and fractions offer two different ways of expressing a value that is not necessarily a whole number but are, in fact, equal in value. One form is not necessarily better than the other since their values are equal. An easy way to demonstrate how closely related fractions are to decimals involves the parts of a dollar. One-half of a dollar is $.50, correct? We know that the fraction ½ is the same as the decimal 0.50. What about one-fourth of a dollar? Isn't that $.25? Aren't one-fourth and 0.25 equal? Don't they have the same value? Of course they do!

In this chapter I will take time to show how you can change a fraction to a decimal and vice versa. However, for the time being, think in terms of money whenever possible. It is actually the easiest way to learn fractions and decimals since we deal with money daily. It is the one common ground we can all easily understand. But also understand that our money system is based upon this relationship. Hopefully this will make the entire process easier for you.

Patterns

As with whole numbers, patterns also help us to see the unique characteristics of each different set of numbers. The characteristics of whole numbers do not necessarily apply to decimals or to fractions. The characteristics of fractions do not necessarily apply to whole numbers or decimals, and so on.

Once again, we are going to look at sequences and use what we know about each set of numbers to help determine the next three terms in the pattern or sequence. When we explored patterns with whole numbers, the possibilities were rather limited. We either added, subtracted, multiplied, or divided to get to the next term. With fractions and decimals, there are many more possibilities beyond the basic operations to get from one term to the next. With this in mind, we first move on to patterns in decimals.

Take a look at each example and see if you can determine what makes up the pattern. Remember that we are not necessarily adding, subtracting, multiplying, or dividing in these cases. Then see if you can apply the pattern to find the next three terms in the sequence.

❶ 0.1, 0.01, 0.001, _____, _____, _____

❷ 1.1, 2.02, 3.003, _____, _____, _____

❸ 9.9, 8.8, 7.7, _____, _____, _____

❹ 777,777.777777, 66,666.66666, 5,555.5555,

_____, _____, _____

❺ 64.64, 32.32, 16.16, _____, _____, _____

Now let's take a look at patterns in fractions. Sometimes these patterns are more difficult to determine. Unlike whole numbers and decimal numbers, fractions have both a numerator *and* a denominator to consider—in other words, a top number (numerator) and a bottom number (denominator) for each term. These two numbers do not necessarily change in the same way in a given sequence. For example, you might have to add to the numerator and subtract from the denominator to complete the sequence. With this in mind, try to determine the next three terms in each of the following sequences:

❻ $\frac{1}{2}$, $\frac{1}{3}$, $\frac{1}{4}$, _____ _____ _____

❼ $\frac{1}{8}$, $\frac{2}{7}$, $\frac{3}{6}$, _____ _____ _____

❽ $\frac{1}{32}$, $\frac{2}{16}$, $\frac{4}{8}$, _____ _____ _____

9 $\dfrac{7}{8}$, $\dfrac{3}{4}$, $\dfrac{5}{8}$, ___ , ___ , ___

10 $\dfrac{1}{2}$, $\dfrac{2}{3}$, $\dfrac{3}{4}$, ___ , ___ , ___

Conversions

The processes we use for changing (or converting) fractions to decimals and decimals to fractions are really quite elementary. What are the easiest ways of recognizing fractions and decimals, the changes as well as their relationships.

First, let's consider changing a fraction to a decimal. In the fraction ⅖, the fraction bar (the line between the 2 and the 5) means "divided by." Technically we can read ⅖ as "two divided by five." The easiest way to change this fractional value into decimal form is to perform the division. If you use a calculator to divide, you would find the correct solution.

Referring to money again, I can show you how to convert such fractions without having to go through the tedious computation. This technique will only work when the denominator of the fraction divides evenly into 100. Using the fraction ⅖, mentally divide the denominator, 5, into 100 (the number of cents in one dollar). The result is 20¢. Mentally, multiply this value by the numerator 2, and the answer is 40¢. Written as a decimal, isn't 40¢ the same as 0.40, or just 0.4? Therefore, 0.4 is the decimal equivalent of the fraction ⅖.

Try this technique on the following fractions to see if it simplifies changing a fraction to a decimal:

❶ $\dfrac{3}{20}$

❷ $\dfrac{23}{50}$

❸ $\dfrac{7}{10}$

❹ $\dfrac{3}{4}$

❺ If you had ⅗ of a dollar and then gave away ⅖ of that amount: (a) How much did you have originally? (b) How much did you give away? (c) How much did you have left?

Unfortunately, the denominator of a fraction will not always divide evenly into 100 as these did. However, there are other helpful techniques that you may use. For example, for fractions with the denominator of 9 there is a unique pattern in the decimal equivalents. Take a look at the table below and see if you can figure out the pattern. Note that the bar over each term indicates a repeating decimal. Only those digits under the bar repeat. For example, $0.\overline{2}$ equals $0.22222.\ldots$

⅑ → $0.\overline{1}$	6/9 → $0.\overline{6}$
2/9 → $0.\overline{2}$	7/9 → $0.\overline{7}$
3/9 → $0.\overline{3}$	8/9 → $0.\overline{8}$
4/9 → $0.\overline{4}$	9/9 → $0.\overline{9}$ or 1
5/9 → $0.\overline{5}$	

One denominator that gives an easily recognized pattern in decimals is 4. For example, each ¼ has a decimal equivalent of 0.25. Therefore, ¾ has the decimal equivalent of 0.25 × 3, or 0.75. For many other fractions, you have no choice but to divide the denominator of the fraction into the numerator to arrive at the decimal equivalent. For instance, the fraction ⁷⁄₁₂ can be made into a decimal by computing 7 ÷ 12, or $12\overline{)7}$. When using paper and pencil to divide, remember that the 12 goes on the outside (the divisor) and the 7 goes on the inside (the dividend)!

Now change the following fractions into decimals:

6 $\dfrac{7}{8}$

7 $\dfrac{4}{9}$

8 $\dfrac{1}{3}$

9 $\dfrac{11}{12}$

10 To the nearest cent, how much money would you have left if you had one dollar, spent ⅗ of that on a newspaper, and lost ½ of the remainder?

The process by which we convert a decimal to a fraction is rather simple. The decimal 0.5 is read "five tenths." We therefore can write it the way we read it, namely ⁵⁄₁₀. The key to this conversion is to know your decimal places.

Just remember that decimal places are the same as whole number places, only in reverse and with a "th" ending. For example, the first place to the right of the decimal point is tenths, the second decimal place is hundredths, the third is thousandths, the fourth is ten-thousandths, and so on. With this in mind, try changing the following decimals into fractions:

⓫ 0.04

⓬ 0.0025

⓭ 0.225

⓮ 0.0008

⓯ In decimal form, what part of a gallon do you have left if you start with 0.84 of a gallon of milk and accidentally spill 0.2 of that amount?

Adding and Subtracting Decimals

Since the basic rules for addition and subtraction of decimals are exactly the same, it makes sense to group these operations together. Simply put, the rule is as follows: First line up the decimal points and then add or subtract, whichever the case may be. Of course, your calculator will do this for you automatically, but what if you don't have one handy? I would like to offer some helpful hints.

Let's assume that you have the following addition problem:

$$23.876 + 5.3 = ?$$

The first thing you need to do is align the decimal points. After doing so, the problem should look like this:

```
  23.876
+  5.3
```

Now you have to admit, in this form it looks a little strange—as if digits are missing from the second number in the problem. Therefore, I advise plugging zeros into every place *after* the decimal point that is vacant. It's not always a good idea to simply bring down the overhanging digits into the answer line. In fact, once you get into subtraction of decimals, this can be disastrous since bringing digits down can give you an incorrect answer. Take a look at the problem now and see if it looks more logical:

```
  23.876
+  5.300
```

Just looking at the problem in this form might put you more at ease, since it did look rather strange the other way. And in decimal subtraction it is imperative to put in those zeros or you're likely to make major mistakes. Take a look at this subtraction problem:

```
  245.3
- 22.6578
```

There is no conceivable way (without a calculator) to subtract these unless you first fill in the top row with zeros. That is, how would you subtract a number from nothing? If you were to bring down the last three digits in the second row, your answer would *not* be correct. This is not what we do when we subtract a number from zero. But when we fill in the top row with zeros we have a problem that looks a little more realistic. Just remember that zeros are only place holders; you can add as many as you like at the end of a decimal number without changing its value. Likewise, you can add zeros in front of a number on the left side of the decimal point. Look at the problem now with its place-holding zeros and see if it looks a little more realistic:

$$\begin{array}{r} 245.3000 \\ -\ 22.6578 \\ \hline \end{array}$$

You can use the strategy we discussed in the last chapter to borrow all the way across in the top row instead of borrowing one digit at a time. From this point on, you would subtract as usual and just bring the decimal point down into your answer.

For practice, see how you do with these decimal addition and subtraction problems:

❶ 26.888 + 4.74

❷ 7.5 + 234.812

❸ 472.3 – 50.733

❹ 911.277 – 28.66

❺ Which of the following yields the greatest result?
28.3 – 7.449 or 15.999 + 5.1

The only situation in addition and subtraction of decimals we have not discussed involves operating on decimal numbers when one of the numbers has no apparent decimal point. Consider this example:

177 + 45.63

Any ideas? Well, let's think about it this way: Isn't $25 the same as $25.00? Therefore, wouldn't 177 be the same as 177.00? Absolutely it would! Now you should know what to do with the problem above. It can be expressed like this:

177.00
+ 45.63
‾‾‾‾‾‾‾

The rule here is simple: When there is no decimal point evident, place the decimal point at the (right) end of the number. That is the only place you can put the decimal point without changing the original value of the number.

With each of the following problems, see if you can place the decimal point where it belongs, and then add or subtract:

6 238 + 34.87

7 619.903 + 47

8 533.187 – 78

9 788 – 166.202

10 When you left home for work, you started with $45 in your wallet. You spent $7.95 for lunch, $.50 for a newspaper, and $12 for gasoline. If there were no other expenses, how much money should you have left when you return home?

Adding and Subtracting Fractions

Fortunately for us, the addition and subtraction of fractions has guidelines similar to those we used for decimals. Once again, the rules for addition are the same as those for subtraction. Unfortunately, with fractions the processes are a little more involved than they are with decimals. However, I will endeavor to make the steps as painless as possible.

First of all, you need to have a common denominator (the bottom number) in the fractions you are adding or subtracting. Once you have a common denominator, you can simply add or subtract the numerators and your problem is solved. However, note that we *never* add or subtract the denominators. They appear again, unchanged, in the denominator of the solution.

The following example should help clarify this for you:

$$
\begin{array}{r}
\frac{5}{9} \\
+ \ \frac{2}{9} \\
\hline
\frac{7}{9}
\end{array}
$$

Now if the fractions you are adding or subtracting have unlike denominators, this is a different story altogether. Arriving at a common denominator is not as difficult as some people make it appear. Let's take a look at the following example and I'll explain how to get the common denominator:

$$\frac{5}{8}$$

$$+ \frac{1}{6}$$

Before we can add these fractions, each must be changed into an equivalent fraction, where both new fractions have the same denominator. To find the least common denominator, you need to find the *smallest* number that both denominators can divide into evenly. In other words, what is the smallest number you can think of that 8 and 6 can both divide into evenly? The answer to this question is 24.

But what if you couldn't come up with this number on your own? The safest way to get a common denominator is to simply multiply the two denominators together. It may not give the *least* common denominator. However, it is not necessary to have the least common denominator to add or subtract. *Any* common denominator will do.

In this case we could multiply 8 and 6 to get the common denominator of 48. This would work to solve this problem. Now that we have found a common denominator, what do we do?

$$\frac{5}{8} \qquad \frac{?}{48}$$

$$+ \frac{1}{6} \qquad \frac{?}{48}$$

We have to convert the numerators as well so that the new fractions have values that are equivalent to the original fractions. To accomplish this, we simply multiply the numerator of each fraction by the denominator of the *other* fraction. In this case we would multiply first 5 by 6, and then 1 by 8. Remember: We multiply each numerator by the denominator of the *other* fraction. The problem should now look like this:

$$\frac{5}{8} \qquad \frac{30}{48}$$
$$+\ \frac{1}{6} \qquad \frac{8}{48}$$

Now that the tough part is over, simply add the two *new* numerators and retain the old denominator like this:

$$\frac{5}{8} \qquad \frac{30}{48}$$
$$+\ \frac{1}{6} \qquad \frac{8}{48}$$
$$\frac{38}{48}$$

You can reduce this answer to lower terms. Although we have not yet discussed this, it is a rather simple process. To reduce a fraction to lowest terms, you must find a whole number other than 1 that divides evenly into *both* the numerator and the denominator. In this particular case, we can divide both numerator and denominator by 2:

$$\begin{array}{cc} \dfrac{5}{8} & \dfrac{30}{48} \\[2mm] +\dfrac{1}{6} & \dfrac{8}{48} \end{array}$$

$$\dfrac{38 \div 2}{48 \div 2} = \dfrac{19}{24}$$

The final answer to this problem is $^{19}/_{24}$. You know it cannot be reduced further since there is no number (other than 1) that will divide evenly into both 19 and 24.

Just to check your ability at reducing fractions, try reducing these to lowest terms:

❶ $\dfrac{12}{36}$

❷ $\dfrac{15}{60}$

❸ $\dfrac{20}{28}$

❹ $\dfrac{30}{48}$

Now, let's get back to adding and subtracting fractions. Test your ability with these problems. Just remember that fractions need to have a common denominator before you add or subtract.

5 $\dfrac{11}{15}$

$+\ \dfrac{7}{15}$

---

6 $\dfrac{5}{8}$

$-\ \dfrac{4}{10}$

---

7 $\dfrac{7}{12}$

$+\ \dfrac{10}{24}$

---

8 $\dfrac{12}{40}$

$-\ \dfrac{14}{60}$

---

9 You are having a dinner party for a group of your friends and need to purchase 6 pounds of steak for the occasion. The three packages you are purchasing have the following weights: 1⅖ pounds, 2⁷⁄₁₀ pounds, and 2 pounds Will this be enough for the occasion?

Multiplying Decimals

The process of multiplying decimals is not a terribly difficult one. Actually, it's a lot easier than adding or subtracting
in that you do not need to line up the decimal points. If you
know how to multiply whole numbers, you can easily multiply decimal numbers. The steps are quite simply these:

    Step 1: Multiply the numbers, ignoring the decimal
                points.
    Step 2: Count the total number of decimal places in
                the problem.
    Step 3: In the product, count off (from right to left)
                the total number of decimal places as in the
                original problem.
    Step 4: Place the decimal point in your answer.

Just remember: It is not necessary to line up the decimal points when you multiply. That applies *only* to addition and subtraction.

Now let's take a look at the following example:

$$233.15$$
$$\underline{\times\quad 3.6}$$

Following the steps outlined above, we first multiply the
numbers, ignoring the decimal points. Notice that I have
used zeros as place holders so all my digits line up:

$$23315$$
$$\underline{\times\quad\quad 36}$$
$$139890$$
$$\underline{699450}$$
$$839340$$

Now count the *total* number of decimal places in the original problem:

$$
\begin{array}{rl}
233.15 & \text{2 decimal places} \\
\times \quad 3.6 & \text{+ 1 decimal places} \\
\hline
& \text{3 decimal places}
\end{array}
$$

Then, counting from right to left, mark off the third decimal place in your answer:

$$
\begin{array}{r}
23315 \\
\times \quad 3.6 \\
\hline
139890 \\
699450 \\
\hline
839.340
\end{array}
$$

The final answer is 839.340, or just 839.34.

Now, try these for practice:

❶ 75.12 × 1.4

❷ 86.6 × 4.3

❸ 90.5 × 2.5

❹ 124.3 × 1.33

❺ Find the total cost of 2.5 pounds of bananas at $0.79 per pound and 1.5 pounds of avocados at $1.29 per pound. (Round each product to the nearest cent before reaching your total, the same as a cash register would do.)

What happens when you are multiplying a decimal number by a whole number? Actually, we have not overlooked this situation at all. You follow *exactly* the same steps as outlined when multiplying a decimal number by a decimal number. The only difference is that the total number of decimal places will depend on the number of decimal places in the decimal number *only*. The whole number displays no actual decimal places, so we count the whole number as having zero decimal places.

Look at this example:

$$
\begin{array}{r}
344.68 \\
\times \quad 23 \\
\hline
103404 \\
689360 \\
\hline
7927.64
\end{array}
$$

Notice that there are only two decimal places in the problem and hence two decimal places in the answer.

Now try these problems. Keep in mind that if your answer ends in one or more zeros on the right side of the decimal point, these can be left off without changing the value of the number.

❻ 323.66 × 26

❼ 1.0248 × 18

❽ 1267.9 × 370

❾ 0.0056 × 45

❿ Barb and Tom are going to the movies with their two children. Brett and Kurt are 8 and 4 years old, respectively. If the cost of tickets is $8.50 for adults and $3.75 for children under twelve, what will be the total ticket cost for this family?

Multiplying Fractions

By comparison, multiplying fractions is much easier than adding or subtracting them. You do not need a common denominator, which in itself is enough to make the process simpler. However, you do need to remember to reduce whenever and wherever possible, as answers are always expressed in lowest terms. There is the process of cross-cancellation (a form of reducing before you solve the problem) that actually makes the multiplication easier. Cross-cancellation reduces the size of the numbers you are working with so that you are less likely to err when you actually multiply.

First, let's take a look at the sample problem below:

$$\frac{12}{30} \times \frac{20}{36} = \quad ?$$

Notice how large the resulting numerator and denominator would be if I could not cross-cancel before multiplying. My answer would still turn out the same if I remembered to reduce at the end, but the numbers to work with would be rather large! To cross-cancel, look at the numerator of one fraction and the denominator of the other fraction. Can you divide both these numbers by any whole number other than 1?

Let's first take a look at 12 and 36. I could divide both of these by 12 and would then be left with 1 and 3. Replace these in your problem like this:

$$\frac{1}{30} \times \frac{20}{3} = \quad ?$$

Now look at 20 and 30. Is there a number other than 1 that would divide evenly into both of these? The largest number that divides both evenly is 10. After dividing both 20 and 30 by 10, we are left with the numbers 2 and 3. Now replace these in your problem and your new problem should look like this:

$$\frac{1}{3} \times \frac{2}{3} = \ ?$$

Now, multiply straight across to get your answer. This is the way to solve this problem now:

$$\frac{1 \times 2}{3 \times 3} = \frac{2}{9}$$

Therefore, your final answer is ⅔.

How about trying a few more problems to see if you get the idea?

❶ $\dfrac{15}{24} \times \dfrac{18}{25}$

❷ $\dfrac{12}{28} \times \dfrac{16}{36}$

❸ $\dfrac{22}{45} \times \dfrac{30}{44}$

❹ $\dfrac{24}{32} \times \dfrac{40}{48}$

❺ At Kennedy High School, ⅘ of the seniors will graduate on time in June. The remaining ⅕ of the seniors will need to attend summer school to complete requirements for graduation. Of those graduating in June, ⅜ will attend state colleges and ⅝ will attend other colleges or join the military. No data is known for the delayed graduates. What fraction of the original senior class do we know will attend state colleges? What fraction will attend other colleges or join the military?

Dividing Decimals

This particular operation on decimals can get tricky and requires very close attention to the problems. In a relatively easy problem of this kind, dividing a decimal number by a whole number, you simply raise the decimal point straight up into your answer. Look at this example and you'll see what I mean:

$372.5 \div 50$

When you set up the problem (assuming you do not have a calculator handy), it should look like this:

$$
\begin{array}{r}
7.45 \\
50{\overline{\smash{)}\,372.50}} \\
\underline{-350} \\
225 \\
\underline{-200} \\
250 \\
\underline{-250} \\
0
\end{array}
$$

Please notice that I brought the decimal point straight up into my answer. Also, notice that I had to add one zero, after the 5 inside, to complete the division. It is appropriate to do so, since adding zeros at the end of the number on the right of the decimal point does *not* change the value of the number. Remember that 5 has the same value as 5.0 or even 5.000.

How about trying a few decimal division problems to see how you do? You can check your answers either by using a calculator or by turning to the answer key in the back of the book.

   ❶ $22\overline{)519.2}$

   ❷ $37\overline{)699.3}$

   ❸ $53\overline{)1293.2}$

   ❹ $75\overline{)3424.5}$

   ❺ **David has $62.50 to spend on Christmas presents for his five brothers and sisters. He wants to spend an equal amount on each sibling. How much, at most, can he spend on each brother and sister?**

When you are dividing a decimal number by another decimal number, the mechanics of the entire problem change. Let's take a look at an example of dividing a decimal by another decimal. I'll simplify the process for you by explaining each step.

First, here's the problem:

$$23.5\overline{)528.75}$$

The first thing you need to know is that you cannot divide the problem the way it is now. When the divisor (the number on the outside) has a decimal point, there is an important step before you begin dividing. You must first change the divisor into a whole number. You do this by moving the decimal point from its current place all the way to the right so that it is up against the fraction frame. In this particular problem, you only need to move the decimal point one place to the right. This step gives us:

$$235\overline{)528.75}$$

However, before you divide, you must also move the decimal point in the dividend (the number inside) the same number of decimal places that you moved it in the divisor. When you do, the problem should now look like this:

$$235\overline{)5287.5}$$

Now that the divisor is a whole number, you can go ahead and divide as we did in the first example of decimal division. That is, move the decimal point straight up into your answer and divide as usual.

By the way, there is a reason for the steps we took. By moving the decimal point one decimal place in both the divisor and the dividend, we were simply multiplying the entire problem by ten, thereby leaving the solution unchanged. In the process, we created a new problem that we could solve based on our knowledge of dividing a decimal by a whole number.

Now let's go ahead and divide this last sample problem and see what answer we get:

$$235\overline{)5287.5} \quad \begin{array}{r} 22.5 \end{array}$$

$$
\begin{array}{r}
22.5 \\
235\overline{)\,5287.5} \\
\underline{-470} \\
587 \\
\underline{-\;470} \\
1175 \\
\underline{-\,1175} \\
0
\end{array}
$$

Now that we have arrived at an answer, let's check to see that this method of dividing decimals works. Remember: To check a division problem, we simply multiply the answer, or quotient, by the divisor. Your answer should be the dividend (the number inside).

Multiply 22.5 (the quotient) by 23.5 (the divisor). Use a calculator if you like. Either way, the result will be 528.75. If you check, you will find that this is the dividend of the original problem!

Now, why don't you try several decimal division problems and see how you do?

❻ $5.2\overline{)45.24}$

❼ $7.7\overline{)89.32}$

❽ $9.6\overline{)117.12}$

❾ $24.5\overline{)1139.25}$

⑩ **The Warner family has a monthly budget of $3,320.50. There are four members of the Warner family. If the average monthly expenditure for each member of the family is $834.25, will the family be able to maintain their monthly budget? Devise a decimal division problem to solve this problem.**

Dividing Fractions

You'll be happy to know that this particular process has fewer steps and fewer complications than dividing decimals. As a matter of fact, you'll be delighted to know that the operation of dividing fractions is so close to multiplying fractions that there is only one additional step to complete the process.

First, you need to remember how to multiply fractions. Once you remember how to multiply, you've got it made. Let's take a look at a division of fractions problem and I'll explain:

$$\frac{3}{5} \div \frac{6}{25}$$

The rule, simply put, is to invert the divisor and multiply. That is, take the second fraction (never the first), switch its numerator and denominator, and then multiply the resulting fractions. When you invert the second fraction and change it to a multiplication problem, our example should look like this:

$$\frac{3}{5} \times \frac{25}{6}$$

Next, cross-cancel (if possible) and multiply. The problem should come out like this:

$$\frac{1}{1} \times \frac{5}{2} = \frac{5}{2} \quad \text{or } 2\frac{1}{2}$$

Now, are you ready to try a few? They really are not difficult at all. Try these:

❶ $\dfrac{12}{15} \div \dfrac{9}{25}$

❷ $\dfrac{11}{18} \div \dfrac{33}{36}$

❸ $\dfrac{20}{32} \div \dfrac{40}{48}$

❹ $\dfrac{27}{50} \div \dfrac{36}{75}$

❺ Barbara has 7⁄8 of a yard of plaid fabric. How many pieces of fabric 7⁄24 yard long can she get out of the 7⁄8 yard that she has?

Now that we have reached the end of the chapter, I again would like to provide you with a review of procedures for quick reference.

CHAPTER CHEAT SHEET

To convert a fraction to a decimal, simply divide.

To convert a decimal to a fraction, read it as a decimal.

Adding and subtracting decimals:
Line up decimal points.

Adding and subtracting fractions:
Find a common denominator.

Multiplying decimals:
Count decimal places.

Multiplying fractions:
Cross cancel; multiply straight across.

Dividing decimals:
Change divisor to whole number first.

Dividing fractions:
Invert second fraction, then multiply.

Next we move into another arena, one that will further test your abilities with decimals and fractions. Percent problems involve both decimals and fractions, so we will constantly be referring back to these particular skills. Read on!

Percents

Of all the mathematical skills one can learn, using percents is probably one of the most useful and practical skills one can acquire. The applications today are limitless. You see them everywhere. Discounts and interest rates are among the most common uses you will recognize. Statistically speaking, they appear in the sports section of the newspaper as batting averages and records of wins versus losses, and for bank certificates (CDs) they indicate interest being paid. Percents are literally everywhere we look. To understand them, no doubt, will make them of greater value to you.

Before we get into the topic of using percents, it is important to first understand exactly what percents mean. To use them successfully, you must first understand the mechanics of percents. You will need to understand first off that percents are based on 100. In other words, 100 percent, which is written as 100%, means "everything" or "all of it" or "the whole thing." Armed with this knowledge, would it not be safe to say that 50% is one-half of everything? Since 50 is exactly one-half of 100, then 50% is one-half of 100%. Simple, right? Therefore, 50%, written as a fraction, is ½.

This is the area in which we are going to begin exploring percents. Changing percents from one form to another allows us to manipulate them and use them in a format that is most convenient for us. Hence, we will first deal with the process of changing percents from one form to another, called *conversions*.

Conversions

To understand percents thoroughly, we first must understand the relationship of percents to other numeric forms. Thus, we begin by exploring the process of changing percents to decimals and then to fractions. Along the way, I will also take the time to explain how we change percents to these other numeric forms.

To change a percent to a decimal, we simply manipulate, or move, the decimal point. We move the decimal point two places. Yes, it's that simple. The trick, however, is to know which way to move it. When changing a percent to a decimal, we *always* move the decimal point two places to the left. The easiest way to remember this at the start is to notice that a percent is usually a whole number and a whole number is always larger than a decimal number. And since we are going from a large number to a small number we move the decimal point left, since moving the decimal point left will also reduce the value of the number. Remember the guideline: two places left. In other words, 50% is equal to 0.50. Keep in mind that the decimal point, though unseen in 50%, was originally at the end of the number, or 50.0%. This conversion is actually a very simple process. The only confusion that might arise happens when the percent is greater than 100 or less than 1 or involves a fraction. Let me explain.

Remember that we said that 50% is equivalent to the decimal number 0.50? We moved the decimal point *exactly* two places. You do the same thing when the percentage is greater than 100. For example: 250% is equivalent to 2.50 or simply 2.5. Notice that the decimal point was moved exactly two places left to change from 250.0% to 2.50. These two numeric expressions are equivalent.

Now let's look at a situation where the percent is less than 1. For example: 0.05% written as a decimal would be 0.0005. Looks confusing? Not really. All we did was move the decimal point two places to the left. Yes, I had to insert zeros to accommodate the repositioned decimal point, but they are merely place holders and have no value here. If you look closely, you will see that we did nothing different than with the other examples. We simply moved the decimal point two places to the left. Remember that changing a value from a percent to a decimal appears to make the number smaller.

Now let's look at an example where there is a fraction as part of the percent. Let's say we have 10½%. There are two different ways to look at this problem. We can leave it as is and move the decimal point two places left as we did in the other examples, which would give us 0.10½, or we can first change the fractional part to a decimal (10.5%) and then move the decimal point two places left, which would give us 0.105. For our purposes, it is best if we change the fraction to a decimal first (the second example) before moving the decimal point.

Now that we have covered all the possible forms of percents, see if you understand the procedure. Change each of the following percents to a decimal. Remember to check your answers against those in the back of the book.

❶ 48%

❷ 15⅛%

❸ 500%

❹ 26.66%

❺ Dale is earning 8¾% interest on his savings account. To find the actual amount of interest he has earned, he will need to change the percent to a decimal. How would you write 8¾% as a decimal number?

Now let's take a look at converting percents to fractions. The process involves changing percents to decimals first. We noted previously that percents are *always* based on 100. Now we are going to apply this information.

If I were to ask you to write 40% as a fraction, you would simply put 40 over 100, since percents are based on 100. For example, 40% written as a fraction would be $^{40}/_{100}$. However, you will need to realize that operating with numbers like this will always be easier if you have your fractions in lowest terms.

If you have forgotten how to reduce fractions to lowest terms, look back to Chapter 2, where you found the largest possible number that divides evenly into both the numerator (top) and the denominator (bottom) of a fraction. For the fraction $^{40}\!/_{100}$, that number would be 20. When you divide both the numerator (40) and the denominator (100) by 20, the resulting fraction is $\frac{2}{5}$. For practical purposes, this lowest-terms fraction is the best answer.

Now, convert these fractions to decimals and see how you do. Always reduce your fractions to lowest terms. Don't forget to check your answers.

⑥ 25%

⑦ 60%

⑧ 39%

⑨ 6%

⑩ Lowell bought 75% of the lumber he needed to build a bookshelf for the family room. What fraction of the total lumber for the project does he still need to purchase? (Lowest terms!)

Now, what happens when you have a percent that is greater than 100%? If you think about it for just a moment, you're likely to figure this out on your own. What will happen is that you will have a mixed number, such as $3\frac{1}{2}$, or you will have a whole number. The reason is that 100% represents exactly 1, so any larger percent will represent a numeric value greater than 1, and possibly a mixed number. Make sense?

Procedurally, nothing really changes. Let's look at 525% as an example. First, you would make a fraction by putting 525 over 100, which gives $^{525}\!/_{100}$. Yes, this fraction is improper, but we can fix that. First, let's reduce it. The largest number that divides evenly into the numerator and the denominator is 25. So, we divide both 525 and 100 by 25 and we end up with $2\frac{1}{4}$. Since this fraction is still improper, we simply divide to get our mixed number. Twenty-one divided by four is five with a remainder of one. Therefore, 5 is our whole number and 1 is the numerator of the remaining fraction. We always place the numerator of the fraction over the divisor (which was 4), so our final answer is $5\frac{1}{4}$. That is, 525% written as a mixed number is $5\frac{1}{4}$.

Do you notice anything unusual about the answer we just got? Did you notice that the hundreds of percent were the whole number in the resulting mixed number? When 500 is subtracted from 525, the remainder is 25, and $\frac{25}{100}$ is the fractional part of the result in its nonreduced form. Let me walk you through an example that makes use of these observations and I'm sure you'll understand.

Let's take 275% and write this as a fraction or mixed number. Notice that 275% is the same as 200% + 75%, correct? You should recognize that 200% written as a decimal number is 2.00, or 2, agreed? And 75% written as a fraction is $\frac{75}{100}$, or $\frac{3}{4}$ when reduced. Add these two parts together, $2 + \frac{3}{4}$, and you will arrive at your answer, $2\frac{3}{4}$. This is the numeric value of 275% written as a mixed number. The easiest way to remember this method is to always write the hundreds of a percent as a whole number and the leftover as a fraction over 100. It's that easy!

Now that you have this down, let's try converting a few larger percentages to see how well you do.

⑪ 150%

⑫ 300%

⑬ 460%

⑭ 725%

⑮ **Beth decided to enlarge a photo of her daughters by 250%. What fraction of the original would the enlargement be?**

The only situation we have not yet discussed is when a percentage is less than 1%. How do we change such a small percentage to a fraction? Let's take 0.5% and write it as a fraction. What you will want to do first is to change the percentage to a decimal value. This is done by moving the decimal point how many places to the left? Two, that's correct. Now we have 0.005, agreed? Look very carefully at what we have written. If you were to read this number according to the decimal placement, wouldn't you read it as five-thousandths? If you were to write a fraction representing exactly what you just read, wouldn't it look like this: $\frac{5}{1000}$? Once you reduce this fraction, your work is done. In its reduced form, you would have $\frac{1}{200}$, the fractional form of 0.5%.

How about trying these conversions? Always remember to reduce your fractions to lowest terms, and then check your answers.

⑯ 0.2%

⑰ 0.75%

⑱ 0.05%

⑲ 0.625%

⑳ Sid decided to reduce the size of a photo so it would fit into a locket. He figured if he reduced each dimension of the photo by 0.8%, it would fit. What fraction of the original length would he be eliminating?

We have discussed converting percents to decimals and to fractions. What if we need to do the reverse—that is, change either a fraction or a decimal to a percent? Here's what we do.

To change a decimal to a percent, you simply move the decimal point two places to the right. This is the *opposite* direction, but the same number of places that the decimal point was moved when converting *from* a percent to a decimal. Just remember that it's always two places that you move the decimal point.

Here's an example to show just how easy it is. Change 0.28 to a percent. Remember to move the decimal two places right. Then you will have 28.0, correct? In other words, 0.28 is the same as 28%. See how easy it is?

Now, you try these and remember to check your answers as you go:

㉑ 0.66

㉒ 0.8

㉓ 0.625

㉔ 0.4

㉕ George wanted to increase his savings account by about 0.55 of its current value. By what percent of his original savings did he wish to increase his savings account?

Now we need to look at the process by which we change a fraction to a percent. Actually, it's pretty simple. There are exactly two steps to this conversion process. First you multiply the numerator of the fraction by 100 and then divide that result by the denominator. Here's how it works.

Let's start with the fraction ⅘. To change this to a percent, we first multiply the numerator, 4, by 100. That result is 400, agreed? Now we take that result, 400, and divide it by the numerator of the original fraction, which is 5. When we divide 5 into 400, the answer is 80. Therefore, ⅘ written as a percent is 80%. Easy enough? How about one more example?

Let's change ⅜ to a percent. First multiply the numerator, 3, by 100. That result, 300, now needs to be divided by the denominator, 8. When we divide, the answer is 37.5 or 37½. Therefore, ⅜ written as a percent is 37½% or 37.5%.

Now let's see how you do with these fractions that we wish to change into percents. Don't forget to check your answers as you go:

26 ¾

27 ⅖

28 ⁷⁄₁₀

29 ⅞

30 **Phyllis spends ¼ of her monthly salary on rent. What percent of her monthly salary does she spend on rent?**

Hopefully, you have reached a point where you are beginning to see the relationship between percents and other numeric values. I know that you are going to find this next section of benefit. This is where you will see why it is so important to know how to change percents to fractions and decimals. We are now going to explore the process by which we solve percent problems.

Percent Problems

Now that we have explored the arena of conversions, we are going to use percents to solve problems. There are many schools of thought on how to solve percent problems, and most of the books that I have ever worked with show different ways to solve different types of percent problems. I have always found it best to keep it as uncomplicated as possible. The underlying theme: Keep it simple. And I'm going to show you how.

My method of solving percent problems involves a very basic formula. It reads, "Is over of equals percent over 100." Now most people will look at this and ask, "What is he talking about?" Actually, it's easy. Look at the formula below:

$$\frac{\textbf{IS}}{\textbf{OF}} = \frac{\textbf{PERCENT}}{\textbf{100}}$$

Here's how it works: In any standard percent problem, the numbers and their locations within the statement of the problem determine their placement in the formula.

Look at this example and I think you'll begin to see what I mean. What is 40% of 250? I am going to attempt to break this problem down, bit by bit, to assist you in placing the numbers in the formula. First, look at the problem, noticing that I have underlined one part: <u>What is</u> 40% of 250? Since "what" is next to "is," this is our unknown part of the problem. In algebra it is customary to use either an n or an x to represent an unknown value such as this.

$$\frac{n}{\text{OF}} = \frac{\text{PERCENT}}{100}$$

Now look at the next part I have underlined in this problem: What is <u>40%</u> of 250? This is the percent; therefore we substitute 40 in place of PERCENT.

$$\frac{n}{\text{OF}} = \frac{40}{100}$$

Now look at the next part I have underlined in the problem What is 40% <u>of 250</u>? So 250 is the OF factor since it is next to the word "of." We substitute 250 in its place in the formula.

$$\frac{n}{250} = \frac{40}{100}$$

If you look closely, you will notice that our proportion is complete except for one detail. We have yet to determine what n is. Finding its value proves to be easy. Take a look at the proportion again:

$$\frac{n}{250} = \frac{40}{100}$$

To begin, cross-multiply where you can. However, do

not multiply n by 100 because you want to keep n by itself on one side of the equation. You can cross-multiply 250 by 40 which gives you 10,000. Next, you divide this by the number left in the denominator. In other words, use each number in the proportion exactly once to solve it. In this problem, when we divide 10,000 by 100, we get 100. Therefore, we now know that 100 is 40% of 250. Did you get it?

Let's try another: 30 is 25% of what number? Using "Is over of," plug the numbers in where they belong. The formula should look like this:

$$\frac{30}{n} = \frac{25}{100}$$

Notice that 30 is next to "is" so it was substituted for IS. Since 25 is the percent in the problem, we substituted it for PERCENT. The 100 in the denominator is called a constant, meaning that it is always used in these problems. And finally, an n was used for OF since that was the one part of the problem for which we did not have a numeric value. At this point, it is also worthwhile to mention that each and every one of these problems will have *exactly one* missing part. It is not possible to solve if there is more than one part of the problem missing.

Now let's go ahead and solve this example:

$$\frac{30}{n} = \frac{25}{100}$$

First, cross-multiply where you can. We would multiply 30 by 100. We take that result, 3000, and divide it by the remaining factor of 25. Our final result is 120. Notice again that each number in the proportion is used only once in the solution process.

Therefore, 30 is 25% of 120. Is that better? I hope so, since you are now going to try several percent problems on your own. To solve them, follow these simple steps:

Step 1: Substitute numeric values in the formula.

Step 2: Cross-multiply where you can.

Step 3: Divide to finish the problem.

Step 4: Make sure that you used each factor only once to reach your solution.

Be sure to check your answers when you have finished working these problems:

❶ What is 30% of 600?

❷ 40 is what percent of 120?

❸ 50 is 25% of what number?

❹ Find 80% of 3000.

❺ What is 56% of 2200?

❻ 255 is what percent of 1275?

❼ 98 is 40% of what number?

❽ Find 36.5% of 1800.

❾ Since 30% of 600 is 180, what do you think 60% of 600 is?

❿ Chris purchased 240 ceramic tiles for his master bathroom. This is 80% of the tiles he needs to complete the job. How many more tiles does he need to order to finish the job?

Discounts

Now that you have an idea as to how percents work, we are going to explore an even more practical application of the subject. It's a very common phenomenon to walk through a shopping mall or into a clothing or department store and see signs everywhere boasting "25% off" or "33⅓% off" or "save up to 50%." Wouldn't it be nice if you could figure approximately what you expect to pay for an item without having to run to the cash register to ask? I will attempt to show you how you can do this mentally with minor difficulty.

First, let's take a look at several basic relationships that will make everything a lot easier to understand. It's important to understand that these are probably the most significant percents you will need to know for discount purposes. Take a look at these percent-to-fraction relationships:

$$20\% \quad = \quad \tfrac{1}{5}$$

$$25\% \quad = \quad \tfrac{1}{4}$$

$$33\tfrac{1}{3}\% \quad = \quad \tfrac{1}{3}$$

$$50\% \quad = \quad \tfrac{1}{2}$$

Notice that each of these fractional equivalents has a numerator of 1. This will actually make the entire process easier. Later I will show you what to do with a fractional equivalent that has a numerator other than 1. For now, let's take a look at the following scenarios:

The local department store is having a sale on jeans. All

jeans are on sale for 25% off. You select a pair of jeans that regularly sell for $39.99. It will be easier to round that figure to $40.00 for discount purposes. Look at the chart above and notice that the fractional equivalent of 25% is ¼. If you divide the denominator of the fraction, 4, into the original price, 40, you will find that it goes 10 times. Thus, 10 is the amount of the discount. Simply subtract that amount from the original price and you will have your sale price of $30.00. Looks easy? It really is.

Let's try another one. You are looking for a new dining room set. The local furniture store is having a store-wide sale with 33⅓% off the prices of all discontinued items. You find a dining room set that regularly sells for $1799.99. About how much could you expect to pay for the set?

First of all, we need to realize that 33⅓% is equivalent to the fraction ⅓. Armed with this information, we would simply divide the denominator, 3, into the approximate selling price of the merchandise, which is $1800. The result of the division is $600. Simply deduct that amount from the original price of the item; the result is about $1200.00. That is approximately what you could expect to pay for the furniture.

Now, what happens in a situation where the discount is not an easy fraction? For example, let's say the discount on an item is 40%. As a fraction, this is equivalent to ⅖. Now what? It will be easier for me to explain if we start with an example.

Let's say you are trying to figure a discount of 40% on an item that originally sells for $300.00. As in the other examples, we still need to divide the original amount by the denominator of the fraction. In other words, we divide

300 by 5. Once you have done that, you simply multiply that quotient, which is 60, by the numerator of the fraction, which in this case is 2. The product, 120, is the actual discount. Does it make sense? Let's try one more and then I'll give you several to try on your own.

Let's say that you are going to be given a discount of 30% on an item originally priced $80.00. The first step involves changing the percent to a fraction. The fractional equivalent of 30% is ³⁄₁₀. (Remember that to change a percent to a fraction, we simply put the percent over 100 and reduce to lowest terms.) Now that we know that 30% is equal to ³⁄₁₀, we divide the denominator, 10, into 80, the original price in dollars. We take that answer, 8, and multiply it by the numerator of the fraction, 3, and our result is 24. Therefore the amount of discount is $24.00. That is *not* the sale price. Rather, we have to deduct that amount from the original price to arrive at the sale price. Subtract 24 from 80 and the result is 56. Therefore the sale price is $56.00.

Now it's your turn to try several similar problems. The first ones are relatively easy so you can adjust to the process, and then we'll see how you do with the more difficult problems. Remember to round off the dollar amounts before you begin!

For each of the following problems, a full price and a discount are shown. You will need to find two answers. First you will want to find the amount of the discount, and then find the sale price. Just remember to check your answers as you go.

❶ $499.99 at 20% off

❷ $119.95 at 33⅓% off

❸ $24.98 at 50% off

❹ $1999.99 at 25% off

❺ $749.98 at 40% off

❻ $19.95 at 10% off

❼ $39.95 at 30% off

❽ $49.98 at 60% off

❾ $349.97 at 80% off

❿ Jeff and Linda have decided to buy a new minivan at the local auto dealership, which has been running an ad in the newspaper. The ad says that all minivans are currently on sale at 33⅓% off the sticker price. Jeff and Linda are most interested in a model that originally sells for $18,700. They also decide to purchase a special options package for the vehicle at a cost of $1200, there is no discount for this package. Before tax and license, about how much should they expect to pay for the minivan?

Percents of Increase and Decrease

Now that we have addressed percent conversions, standard percent problems, and discounts, we are left to deal with percents of increase and decrease. This includes but is not limited to markup and selling price. If you are interested in knowing how much the value of a piece of real estate has increased or decreased during a certain period of time, or if you would like to know how much a collector's plate has increased in value over a period of years, percents of increase and decrease can assist you in finding the answers.

Though such problems involve an additional formula, the good news is that this formula is not vastly different from the "Is over of" formula. Take a look at the formula below and I will explain exactly how it works:

$$\frac{\textbf{DIFFERENCE}}{\textbf{ORIGINAL}} = \frac{\textbf{PERCENT}}{\textbf{100}}$$

Let's begin with an example that uses this format and which will help you to see exactly how this formula works. The price of an item is marked up from $20.00 to $25.00. What percent was the item marked up?

First, you would need to identify the *difference* between the two prices. Then you would need to identify the *original* price. Finally, you would substitute these numeric values and solve the proportion as we did in the previous percent problems.

When you have substituted the numeric values, your proportion should look like this:

$$\frac{5}{20} = \frac{n}{100}$$

Please note that the percent *(n)* is our unknown factor here. This is what we will be solving for. The steps are exactly the same as those used in previous problems. First, you cross-multiply where you can. So, we multiply 5 by

100. We then take the result, 500, and divide it by the remaining term, 20. The result, 25, represents the percent of change. The reason that I say "percent of change" is that the value may represent an increase or a decrease; this is completely dependent on whether the difference represents an increase or a decrease. In this particular problem, the price increased from 20 to 25; therefore the result is a percent of increase. Had the situation been reversed, you would have solved the problem the same way, except that you would have used 25 as the original price and the resulting percent of change would have represented a percent of decrease. In other words, the same process is used whether the problem describes an increase *or* a decrease.

Now let's try another example to see that you understand the process. An item is marked down from $50 to $40. Find the percent of increase or decrease. The first step is to find the difference between the two prices. Then you need to identify the original price. Next you substitute the necessary values and operate on the proportion.

Once you have identified the necessary terms for the proportion and have substituted them in, it should look like this:

$$\frac{10}{50} = \frac{n}{100}$$

Hopefully, if you're trying this along with me, you have arrived at the same proportion so far. The next step is to solve the proportion. First multiply 10 by 100. Next, divide that result, 1000, by the remaining term, 50. Your final result is 20. Now we know the percent of change is 20%.

Now we need to determine if this is a percent of increase or decrease. Just take a look back at the original problem and you will see that the answer is quite obvious, it is definitely a 20% decrease since the price was dropped from $50 to $40.

Now, how about trying several of these on your own. Just remember to substitute first and then solve. Also, remember to check your answers against those in the back of the book.

❶ $100 to $60

❷ $30 to $50

❸ $15 to $30

❹ $250 to $400

❺ $300 to $500

❻ The local stationery store purchased pens from their distributor at a cost of $0.08 each. They marked them up to $0.19 each. What was the percent of markup for the pens?

❼ Evan attended an auction where he purchased baseball cards for resale. Some were collector's cards and others were newer sets. One of the newer sets of baseball trading cards he purchased cost him $17.95. He later decided to sell this set for $29.99. To the nearest whole percent, what was the percent of markup on the baseball cards?

There is one more topic relative to percent that we need to address. This topic is interest. Actually, there are two different types of interest that I need to cover with you. Read on.

Simple Interest

Most real-world interest problems involve the calculation of compound interest, which we will explore in the next session. But to begin, we consider simple interest in order to establish an understanding of the concept of interest and how it works.

The concept of simple interest works this way. Let's say you have a savings account in a bank that pays interest only on an annual basis. What happens, basically, is that the bank uses that percentage of interest to calculate how much money to add to your account each year. This formula shows how to calculate simple interest:

Interest = Principal × Rate × Time

In English, this means you multiply the principal (amount in the account) by the rate of interest (in decimal form) multiplied again by the time (the number of years). It actually is a very "simple" process. Let me give you an example.

Let's say you have $1500 in a savings account that pays 6½% simple interest, and you want to know how much interest (in dollars) you will earn in 5 years. First, substitute the appropriate numeric values into the formula, like this:

Interest = 1500 × 0.065 × 5

Notice that I changed the rate, 6½%, into a decimal as is required in this formula. (Remember that ½ is the same as 0.5.) My next step would be to (simply) multiply the values together. One special note here: Multiplication is a commutative process. This means that you can multiply the numbers in *any* order and still arrive at the same answer. This applies to any problem as long as it is *all* addition or *all* multiplication only. Since our problem is all multiplication, we can multiply the numbers in any order that we choose. The reason that I wanted you to know this is I have always found it easiest to multiply certain numbers together first. In our example problem, I would first multiply the 1500 and the 5 together since we can do that part mentally. Next, I would multiply that answer, 7500, by 0.065 to arrive at my final answer of 487.5. The answer tells us that at the end of 5 years, you would have earned $487.50 interest. Does that look easy enough?

Here's one more example before I give you several of your own interest problems to try. Let's say you have $3000 in a savings account that pays 7¼% interest annually. How much interest would you earn in 18 months? Our first step is to substitute numeric values into the formula. It should look like this:

$$\text{Interest} = 3000 \times 0.0725 \times 1.5$$

Notice that I first changed the interest rate into a decimal and the time into the mixed number of years. I changed 7¼% in two steps. First, 7% is the same as 0.07, true? Isn't ¼ of one dollar $0.25? That's where the 0.0725 came from. Remember too that 18 months is 1½ years, which is easier to use in decimal form here since the other numbers in the formula are in decimal form as well. And now that I have plugged everything in, I just multiply to finish the problem.

I would first multiply 3000 by 1.5 since I can do this mentally. Since ½ of 3000 is 1500, 1 times 3000 plus ½ times 3000 would be 4500. Now I multiply this answer, 4500, by 0.0725. For this step I would recommend your calculator. The final answer, $326.25, represents the interest earned after 18 months (or 1½ years). Got it?

Now here are several simple interest problems for you to try on your own. Remember that you can multiply numbers together in any order you desire and it will not affect your answer. And remember to check your answers in the back of the book.

❶ $300 at 8% for 2 years

❷ $1600 at 6¾% for 5 years

❸ $5000 at 5.2% for 6 months

❹ $750 at 7⅜% for 2½ years

❺ Michael has a savings account with a current balance of $785.18 that earns 5¾% simple interest annually. To the nearest cent, how much interest would he earn in two years?

Now that you have a basic understanding of how simple interest works, I would like to introduce you to compound interest. The situations are as different as night and day.

Compound Interest

Simple interest refers to interest that is totaled at the end of a cycle, whereas compound interest is computed periodically. For each period, an increasing amount of compound interest is added to the growing value of an account. I will first show you how to figure this mechanically so you have a clear understanding of how the concept works and then I will show you a formula that puts it all together.

Let's consider a sample problem: Dennis has $500 in a savings account that pays 6% interest and is compounded quarterly. How much interest will he have after one year?

Notice that there are several things going on here. The easiest approach is to look at the problem as a simple interest problem. The original problem states that the interest is compounded (computed) quarterly (every 3 months, or ¼ year). Let's begin solving the problem this way:

$$\text{Interest} = 500 \times 6\% \times \tfrac{1}{4}$$

Next we will change everything to decimals:

$$\text{Interest} = 500 \times 0.06 \times 0.25$$

Notice that I changed the rate (6%) to a decimal, and then I changed 3 months to ¼ year and finally to 0.25, the decimal equivalent of ¼. Now I can multiply the numeric values together to arrive at my answer. The product, when completed, is $7.50. This represents the amount of interest earned during the first quarter, or first 3 months. Now I need to add this into the account to arrive at a new account balance. So I add $500.00 and $7.50. The new account balance is $507.50.

Step two involves the same computation, using the new account balance. We substitute into the same formula as follows:

Interest = 507.50 × 0.06 × 0.25

This will allow us to compute the interest for the second quarter—that is, for months 4, 5, and 6. When computed, the result is 7.6125. The problem here is obvious. We cannot use this figure as it is; we need to round it to the nearest cent. The interest, when rounded, will be $7.61. This is the interest earned for the second quarter. We now add this amount to the previous balance of $507.50 and arrive at the new account balance of $515.11.

We need to follow these same procedures for the next two quarters to complete the process. For the third quarter, we compute as follows:

Interest = 515.11 × 0.06 × 0.25

The result of this multiplication problem is 7.72665. Again we round to the nearest cent before adding to the account balance. That is, 7.72665 rounded to the nearest cent is $7.73, which we add to the previous account balance of $515.11. The new account balance at the end of the third quarter is $522.84.

Finally, we need to compute the interest for the fourth and last quarter. Using the new account balance of $522.84, we substitute into the formula and compute the fourth quarter's interest:

Interest = 522.84 × 0.06 × 0.25

Once again, when we compute, we are going to have a result that needs to be rounded to the nearest cent. When multiplied, our result is 7.8426, which rounds to $7.84. This represents the interest for the fourth quarter. We add this to the previous balance of $522.84. Thus the balance at the end of the fourth quarter is $530.68.

This method that we just completed is the *long* way of computing compound interest. Most people would ask why we just don't use the simple interest formula. To answer this, let me compute for you the results of this previous problem using the simple interest formula so you can compare the results. Substituting the original values into the simple interest formula:

$$\text{Interest} = 500 \times 0.06 \times 1$$

When we have finished multiplying the three numeric terms together, we arrive at 30 as an answer. This represents the simple interest earned at the end of 1 year. Added into the account, the new balance at the end of the year would be $530.00.

Now, compare this to the compound interest balance of $530.68. Granted, the difference is not substantial, but a larger sum of money invested over a longer period of time would most definitely yield a larger amount of interest.

Is there a method by which we might reduce the number of steps needed to find compound interest, such as were needed in our example? Recall that we had to compute the amount of interest for each of four periods.

Just imagine the process we might go through for a problem, let's say, involving interest compounded quarterly over a period of 20 years. Literally, we would have to solve this problem 80 times in order to finish computing all the compound interest earned within that period of time.

In fact, there is a more direct method. It involves a formula more complicated than anything we have dealt with up to this point, but is still a much easier way of computing compound interest. Here is the compound interest formula:

$$A = P[1 + (0.01r/n)]^{nt}$$

This formula looks rather complicated, but it really is not as tough as it seems. We're going to try an example, but first I am going to take a moment to define each of the unknown values. Use the chart below to refer to each of the unknowns:

A = principal + interest
P = principal
r = rate of interest
n = number of times each year the interest is compounded
t = time (in years)

I think you will begin to see how the formula works as we solve this sample problem: Beth invests $3600 in a bank account paying 8% interest compounded quarterly. How much is in the account at the end of 3 years?

First, we will want to substitute all the numeric values in their appropriate places:

$$A = 3600 [1 + (0.01 \times 8/4)]^{(4 \times 3)}$$

Now we will walk through the steps to solve the problem. First, using a calculator, I would multiply 0.01 by 8 and then divide by 4. To the right of the brackets, I would also multiply the 4 and the 3, the two factors of the exponent. The problem would now look like this:

$$A = 3600 \, [1 + 0.02]^{12}$$

Next, I would combine the 1 and the 0.02 and take this sum to the twelfth power (in other words, multiply it by itself twelve times). Now my problem should look something like this:

$$A = 3600 \, [1.26824]$$

I have taken the liberty of rounding the bracketed number to five decimal places, so the problem doesn't go on for days. Now the final step is to multiply 1.26824 by 3600. That result, 4565.67045, needs to be rounded to the nearest cent. My final answer, $4565.67, is the amount of principal and interest combined in the account.

And now for those of you daring enough to risk it, here are several compound interest problems to try. In the back of the book, I have not only listed the answers, but also how the problems should be set up so you can check to see if your work is correct to that point. Just remember to substitute values into the formula first, before you try to solve each problem.

❶ $5000 at 6% compounded annually for 10 years

❷ $4000 at 8% compounded semiannually for 5 years

❸ $8000 at 7½% compounded quarterly for 3 years

❹ $10,000 at 5¾% compounded annually for 6 years

❺ What amount must be invested at 8% compounded quarterly to be worth $6000 after 10 years?

So much for percents. Now you might see how useful and practical the basic knowledge of percents can be. Often times, we don't realize the significance of something until it is pointed out to us. That is what I have attempted to do.

And once again, I am providing you with a review of the skills addressed in this chapter:

CHAPTER CHEAT SHEET

To change:
  Percent to decimal: Move decimal point two places left.
  Percent to fraction: Place % over 100 and reduce.

Standard percent problems:
  Use formula: IS/OF = PERCENT/100

Discounts: Change percent to decimal and multiply.

Percents of increase and decrease:
  Use formula: DIFFERENCE/ORIGINAL = PERCENT/100

Simple interest formula:
  Interest = Principal × Rate × Time (years)

Compounded interest formula:
  $A = P[1 + (0.01r/n)]^{nt}$

Now that we have completed this section, we proceed in another direction. Algebra, an abstract math form, uses all of your basic math skills and puts them to work. Success in algebra depends tremendously on one's mastery of the basic skills. You may be surprised how different the math may appear, yet you will also be surprised how much it really stays the same.

Algebra

Once you have entered the realm of algebra, you begin to understand why you have learned all the basic math skills. You also begin to get a more global picture of the many uses of math, more so than you could with only basic math skills. The most practical use of algebra is problem solving. Algebra teaches you to logically and systematically solve problems once you have assessed a situation. Comparing basic math to algebra is rather easy. Basic math involves learning all the fundamental skills, whereas algebra involves using those skills to solve problems.

In order to effectively use algebra in a problem-solving format, it is necessary to discuss several preliminary skills. The most fundamental skills involve operations with integers.

Just in case you don't remember, an integer is a whole number value (no fractions or decimals, please) that can be positive or negative. This group of numbers does include zero, although zero is neither positive nor negative. As a matter of fact, zero is the only integer that does not carry a sign with it. All other integers can be identified as positive or negative. Zero cannot.

Operations with Integers

To effectively use integers, it is imperative to know all the rules regarding integer operations. Most books and teachers will initiate this discussion with the addition and subtraction of integers. My feeling is that since those operations have the more complicated rules, let's leave them for last. Let's begin with multiplication and division. The rules for multiplying and dividing integers are very easy.

The first rule is this: In multiplication *and* division of integers, if the signs are the same, the result will be positive. If the signs are different, the result will be negative. Let's take a look at several examples so that we can be certain you are getting this.

$$\textit{Example 1:} \quad -4 \times +5 = -20$$

$$\textit{Example 2:} \quad +6 \times -3 = -18$$

$$\textit{Example 3:} \quad +7 \times +4 = +28$$

$$\textit{Example 4:} \quad -2 \times -8 = +16$$

$$\textit{Example 5:} \quad -9 \times 0 = 0$$

Notice that in Examples 1 and 2, the signs of the two factors are different. In each case you have one positive and one negative integer. Notice that the result in each case is negative. Why? Because the signs in the original problem are different. Now in Examples 3 and 4, the signs of the two factors are the same. Example 3 has two positive integers and Example 4 has two negative integers. In both cases, the result is positive. Why? Because the signs in the original problem are the same, as we discussed.

Example 5 is actually the easiest one to explain. Simply put, anything multiplied by zero will *always* equal zero.

At this point, it is also important to mention that positive integers do not necessarily require a + sign in front of them. Understand that "+8" means the same thing as "8." However, a minus sign *is* needed to identify a negative integer. That is, a negative integer must *always* have − in front of it.

Now here are several simple problems to test your ability in multiplying and dividing integers. Don't forget to check your answers in the back of the book. Please note that parentheses imply multiplication when no other operation is indicated outside the parentheses. Parentheses can also be used to separate integers so that you don't confuse the signs. Now try these:

❶ (−12) (−9)

❷ (25) (−8)

❸ (9) (+40)

❹ (−15) (+6)

❺ (−12) (0)

❻ (−4) (−3) (5) (−2)

❼ (8) (−3) (2) (−1)

❽ (6) (−2) (−1) (3)

❾ (−14) (−2) (3) (−5) (−1) (0)

❿ (11) (−2) (4) (−25)

The rules for determining the sign of the result in a division problem are almost identical to the rules for multiplication. When you divide two integers with the same sign, the answer is positive. When you divide two integers with different signs, the answer is negative. Just remember to divide the integers instead of multiplying them. Simple enough? Look at these examples of integer division and then we'll try several for practice.

Example 6: $\quad -50 \div -10 = +5$

Example 7: $\quad +40 \div \quad +8 = +5$

Example 8: $\quad -45 \div \quad +9 = -5$

Example 9: $\quad +75 \div -15 = -5$

Example 10: $\quad 0 \div -20 = \quad 0$

As I mentioned before, the rules are the same as with multiplication. Notice Example 10. Once again we are faced with a problem with zero. Where zero is being divided by some other number, the answer will *always* be zero.

By now, integer division should be getting pretty easy for you. Here are several problems for you to try. Once again, check your answers against those in the back of the book:

⑪ $-88 \div -4$

⑫ $+49 \div -7$

⑬ $100 \div +20$

⑭ $-75 \div 25$

⑮ $(-22)\,(-4) \div (8)$ (*Hint:* Operate from left to right.)

⑯ $(25)\,(-4) \div (5)$ (*Hint:* Operate from left to right.)

⑰ $(100) \div (-5)\,(4)$ (*Hint:* Operate from left to right.)

Now that we have multiplication and division of integers out of the way, let's deal with addition and subtraction. We'll start with addition. The first case we consider is when the signs of the numbers in the problem are the same.

When you are adding two positive integers or two negative integers, the rule is as follows: Disregard the sign for a moment, add the integers together, and assign the same sign to your answer. In other words, if you are adding -5 and -7, your answer would be -12. Or, if you are adding $+4$ and $+6$, your answer would be $+10$, or just 10. This part is easy.

Here are several problems for you to try. When you have finished, check your answers against those in the back of the book. Pay particular attention to the positive and negative signs in your answers.

⑱ $+12 + +16$

⑲ $-42 + -19$

⓴   +35 + +26

㉑   +48 + +55

㉒   −28 + −16

When adding two integers that have unlike signs, there is a different rule to use. If you are adding one positive and one negative integer, you actually subtract first. That is, find the *difference* between the integers as though they both were positive, then give the sign of the larger integer to your result. Let me demonstrate:

Example 11:   +8 + −5 = +3

Example 12:   −7 + +3 = −4

Notice that we first subtracted. In Example 1, we first found the difference between 8 and 5, which is 3. Then we looked at the original problem to see which digit was larger. Since 8 is larger than 5, we take the sign of the 8, which is positive, and give that to our answer. Therefore, our answer is +3.

Now take a look at the second example. First we found the difference between 7 and 3. The result, 4, is assigned the sign of the larger digit from the original problem. Therefore, the final answer is −4.

Now, here are several examples for you to try on your own. Be sure to check your answers when you are finished and pay special attention to the positive and negative signs in the problems.

㉓   +12 + −18

㉔   − 16 + +20

㉕   +28 + −43

㉖   − 33 + +52

㉗   +64 + −44

Now that you have tried both like and unlike signs in addition problems, here are several problems of both types. Pay careful attention to the signs so you know whether to add or subtract and how to determine the appropriate sign for the answer. Remember to check your answers against those in the back of the book.

㉘   +49 + −28

㉙   − 38 + −49

㉚   − 53 + +88

㉛   +71 + −38

㉜   +52 + +90

Now that we have seen how to add integers, let's explore how to subtract integers. I have always found it easier to use a method that involves converting the subtraction problem to an addition problem, and then applying the addition methods we have explored. This process is called "Copy Change Change" (CCC). Let me explain how it works.

First of all, CCC refers to the positive and negative signs in the problem. Let me demonstrate. Take a look at this example.

Example 13: $+43 - -18$

Using CCC, we copy (C) the first sign ($+$), change (C) the second sign ($-$), and change (C) the third sign ($-$). Rewritten, the problem now should look like this

$$+43 + +18$$

Notice that the first sign remained positive. The second sign was changed from a negative to a positive. The third sign was changed from a negative to a positive. Now, we have an addition problem. We refer to our rules for addition to reach the solution:

$$+43 + +18 = +61$$

Let's take a look at another subtraction problem.

Example 14: $-27 - +43$

Using CCC (Copy Change Change), we rewrite the problem to make it addition. It should look like this:

$$-27 + -43$$

Finally, we solve it by using the rules for addition. Since both numbers are negative, we add them together and give the same sign to the answer:

$$-27 + -43 = -70$$

Now, here's your chance to try a few problems on your own. Remember to first rewrite each problem as an addi-

tion problem by using CCC. Then use the rules for addition
to solve:

㉝　−15　−　−27

㉞　+53　−　+26

㉟　−44　−　+49

㊱　+61　−　−19

㊲　−82　−　−44

Now let's put it all together. See if you can solve addition and subtraction problems when they are in a mixed format. Try to solve these problems without referring back to the rules, and remember to check your answers against those in the back of the book.

㊳　−57　+　−84

㊴　+62　−　−25

㊵　−40　+　+38

㊶　+71　+　−23

㊷　−22　−　+46

㊸　+18　+　+53

㊹　−73　−　−28

㊺　+61　−　+48

㊻　−92　+　−47

㊼　+89　+　−63

Following the exploration of integers, we turn our attention to equations and how we solve them. An equation is a mathematical statement with an equal sign. Algebraic equations are identified when we use variables. "$n + 43 = 57$" is one such equation. Notice, there is a variable, n, and an equal sign. Solving an algebraic equation involves finding one or more values of the variable that make the equation true.

Solving Equations

The key to solving any equation is to use the opposite operation. In other words, if you are solving an addition equation, use subtraction. If you are solving a subtraction equation, use addition. If you are solving a multiplication equation, use division. If you are solving a division equation, use multiplication.

Let me give you several examples and demonstrate how to solve them.

Example 1: $n + 35 = 52$

Since this is an addition equation, the opposite operation that we use to solve it is subtraction. The equal sign tells you that the value on its left is exactly the same as the value on its right. So, if you want to subtract from one side of the equation, you must subtract from both sides of the equation to keep it in balance.

Now that we know that we want to subtract, we need to know what to subtract. Since the original equation says to add 35 to the variable, we do the opposite, which is to subtract 35 *from both sides* of the equation. It should now look like this:

$$
\begin{array}{rcr}
n \ + \ 35 & = & 52 \\
- \ 35 & & - \ 35 \\
\hline
n & = & 17
\end{array}
$$

Notice that we subtracted 35 from each side of the equation. On the left side, the $+35$ and the -35 canceled each other. On the right side, 52 minus 35 equals 17. In this equation, the solution is $n = 17$.

To check your solution, you can simply substitute the number you found in place of the variable and you should have a true statement. In other words, we substitute 17 in place of n, which gives us:

$$17 \ + \ 35 \ = \ 52$$

Is this a true statement? Yes it is, so we know that we have arrived at the correct solution.

Now, let's try a subtraction equation. Just remember that we are going to proceed the same way as we did with the addition equation. I'll explain as I demonstrate:

Example 2: $a \ - \ 26 \ = \ 18$

Once again, you will need to remember to operate on both sides of the equation. And since this is a subtraction equation, we will need to use the opposite operation, addition, to solve. Therefore, we are going to add 26 to both sides of the equation. It should look like this:

$$
\begin{array}{r}
a \; - \; 26 \; = \quad 18 \\
+ \; 26 \quad + \; 26 \\
\hline
a \qquad\quad = \quad 44
\end{array}
$$

Notice that the -26 and the $+26$ canceled each other on the left side of the equation. On the right side, 18 plus 26 equals 44. Therefore, the solution is $a = 44$.

To check our answer, we simply substitute the value 44 in place of the variable and see if we have a true statement.

When we substitute the solution in place of the variable, it should look like this:

$$
44 \; - \; 26 \; = \; 18
$$

Is this a true statement? Yes, it is, so this solution is correct.

Now that you've had an opportunity to see an example of an addition equation and a subtraction equation, why don't you try several to see how you do? Remember to check your answers against those in the back of the book.

❶ $c + 39 = 55$

❷ $b - 18 = 71$

❸ $n + 26 = 17$

❹ $f - 14 = -22$

❺ $z + 57 = -33$

Now that we have addressed addition and subtraction equations, we need to take a look at multiplication and division equations. The nice thing is that the procedure is the same. Once again, we use the opposite operation to solve. For example, if we are solving a multiplication equation, division solves the problem. If we are solving a division equation, multiplication solves the problem.

Take a look at these examples and see if you can follow along.

Example 3: $5n = 40$

Since this is a multiplication equation, we use division to solve. It is important to realize here that $5n$ is the same as "5 times n." This should make the procedure a little easier to understand.

We are going to divide both sides of this equation by 5. Rewritten, it should look like this:

$$\frac{5n}{5} = \frac{40}{5}$$

Now that we have rewritten the problem including the reverse operation, all we need to do is solve. When we divide the left side, the 5's cancel and we are left with only the variable n. On the right side we have $40 \div 5 = 8$. So we are now left with 8 on the right side. Our final answer is $n = 8$.

Just as with the addition and subtraction equations, we need to check the solution here for accuracy. Once again, we substitute the value 8 in place of the variable and see if it makes a true statement. Rewritten, the equation should look like this:

$$(5)\,(8)\;=\;40$$

Is this a true statement? Yes, it is, so we know that 8 is a correct value for the variable in the equation.

The final example involves division. Again, we will need to only use the opposite operation to solve. Take a look at this example and I'll explain:

Example 4: $\dfrac{b}{12}\;=\;7$

When you look at this equation, you should read it this way "*b* divided by 12 equals 7." Notice that the fraction bar really means "divided by." And since this is a division equation, we will multiply to solve it. We are going to multiply both sides of the equation by 12 since 12 is the divisor of the variable.

Rewritten, the equation should look like this:

$$\frac{b}{12}\;\times\;\frac{12}{1}\;=\;7\times12$$

Now, granted, in this form the equation looks a little funny. But when we operate, you will notice that the 12's on the left side cancel each other, leaving *b* over 1, which is the same as *b*. On the right side, however, you will have the result of multiplying 7 and 12, which is 84. Therefore, the solution is *b* = 84.

Once again, to check your answer, you simply substitute 84 in place of the variable. It should look like this:

$$\frac{84}{12} = 7$$

This checking can be read as "84 divided by 12 equals 7." Is this a true statement? The answer is yes, so our solution is correct. If for some reason this part of the process did not work, we would know that we had made an error while solving the original problem.

Now, here are several multiplication and division equations for you to try. Be sure to use the opposite operation to solve and also to check your answers as you go.

6 $12\,n = 144$

7 $\dfrac{y}{8} = 18$

8 $24\,f = 312$

9 $\dfrac{z}{15} = 37$

10 $32\,c = 400$ (*Hint:* **Your answer could be a fraction!**)

Now that you have tackled equations with one step, let's see how you can handle equations that require more than one step. There really is not much difference in the process; it's just a little longer. Let me demonstrate with an example. See if you can follow along.

Example 5: $3\,n - 17 = 19$

This is a two-step equation. It's relatively simple to identify it as such since there are exactly two numbers on the same side of the equal sign as the variable. There are a 3 that multiplies the variable and a 17. Each number requires exactly one step to eliminate.

To begin, we need to eliminate the number that is furthest from the variable on the same side of the equal sign. Which of the two numbers, 3 or 17, is furthest from the variable? I hope you responded "17." That is the number we need to eliminate first. Since the original equation is subtraction, we use addition as the opposite operation. So the first step toward our solution should look like this:

$$\begin{array}{rcr} 3n - 17 &=& 19 \\ + 17 && + 17 \\ \hline 3n &=& 36 \end{array}$$

Notice that the -17 and the $+17$ cancel each other. We now have a new equation, $3n = 36$. This part of the problem should look vaguely familiar. It is simply a multiplication equation, so we divide to solve. The second step should look like this:

$$\frac{3n}{3} = \frac{36}{3}$$

Now to complete we simply divide. When we do, we are left with $n = 12$. That should be our solution, but to be safe, we really should substitute the value, 12, in place of the variable to see that it makes a true statement.

When we substitute 12 in place of n, our equation should look like this:

$$3\,(12) \;-\; 17 \;=\; 19 \quad \text{or}$$
$$36 \;-\; 17 \;=\; 19$$

Is this a true statement? Yes, it is. Therefore, our answer $n = 12$ is a correct answer.

Here's one more example for you to observe before I have you try several on your own. Take a look at this example and see if it doesn't make more sense now that you've seen one:

Example 6: $\quad 5\,b \;+\; 23 \;=\; 58$

From the previous example, recall that you would first want to eliminate the 23. To do this, you would subtract 23 from both sides of the equation. It should then look like this:

$$
\begin{array}{rcl}
5\,b \;+\; 23 & = & 58 \\
-\; 23 & & -\; 23 \\
\hline
5\,b \;\;\;\;\;\; & = & 35
\end{array}
$$

You can use division to solve the new equation. Your final step should look like this:

$$\frac{5\,b}{5} \;=\; \frac{35}{5}$$

To reach the solution, we simply divide both sides of the equation by 5. The end result is $b = 7$.

Once again, we need to verify accuracy by substituting our solution value into the original equation. The check should look like this:

$$5\,(7) + 23 = 58 \quad \text{or}$$
$$35 + 23 = 58$$

Since our verification is accurate, we now know that our answer is correct. I hope that this second example has helped solidify the process in your mind so that you are ready to tackle a few algebraic equations on your own. Now let's try several to see how you do. Just remember these easy steps:

Step 1: Use the opposite operation to eliminate the number that is furthest from the variable but on the same side of the equal sign as the variable.

Step 2: Use the opposite operation to eliminate the remaining number so the variable is left alone.

Step 3: Be sure that you are operating on *both* sides of the equal sign in every equation that leads to your solution.

Now, here are your equations to solve. Don't forget to check your answers against those in the back of the book as you go:

⑪ $6f + 48 = 108$

⑫ $7k - 36 = 62$

⑬ $12r + 59 = 191$

⑭ $15g - 78 = 147$

⑮ $427 + 11j = 548$

Also remember to substitute your solution values in place of the variables in the original equations to see that you have accurately solved each equation. If, perchance, you have not, try the problem again to see if you can correctly solve the equation on the second try. Substituting solution values is the safest and quickest way of verifying your answers.

Problem Solving

Now that we have explored the topic of algebraic equations, let's take a look at the practical side of equations. In a problem-solving format, equations are usually the easiest way to interpret problems and to solve them. That is, you will first want to write an equation for the problem before you attempt to solve it. To do this, I utilize a method called **VESA**. This acronym represents the following:

V After you have read the problem, you must first identify the **V**ariable.

E After you have identified the variable, you must then write an **E**quation.

S Once you have written an equation, you must then **S**olve the equation.

A After you have solved your equation, you must then **A**nswer the question. More times than not, the solution to the equation is not exactly the answer to the problem.

Remember **VESA** and the entire process will be much easier for you. Now I am going to demonstrate two examples to help you understand the procedure. The first example is a basic number problem and the second involves a real-life situation. Watch carefully and pay special attention to the methods I employ as we go. Here's our first problem:

> *Example 1:* A number multiplied by seven and then increased by twelve is sixty-eight. What is the number?

Based on **VESA**, the first step would be to write an equation for the problem. Let's take a closer look at the original problem. It will be much easier if we take the problem in smaller pieces.

First we need to identify a **V**ariable. I will use n to represent the number.

Then we will need to write an **E**quation based on the given information. Let's take a look at the first part of the problem: "A number multiplied by seven." To begin writing this in equation form, we would write this as $7n$, where we are using n to represent the number.

The next part of the problem, "increased by twelve," can be written as $+\ 12$. Just to keep this in perspective, "decreased by twelve" would be written as $-\ 12$.

The last part of the problem, "is sixty-eight," can be written as $= 68$. When we put it all together, it should look like this:

$$7n\ +\ 12\ =\ \ \ \ 68$$

Now we **S**olve the equation as we did in the previous section. Watch how I solve the entire equation:

$$7n + 12 = 68$$
$$\underline{ - 12 \quad - 12}$$
$$7n \qquad = 56$$

$$\frac{7n}{7} = \frac{56}{7}$$

$$n = 8$$

Now that we have solved the equation, we need to look at the original problem to determine the answer. It is very important to be certain that we are answering the question we are being asked.

The original problem states: "A number multiplied by seven and then increased by twelve is sixty-eight. What is the number?" In this case, the answer to the problem is simply the solution to the equation, namely the number 8.

Now let's take a look at a situation that will use an equation to answer a question. Though it is a little different from a number problem, it will basically need the same procedures to be solved.

> *Example 2:* Jesse has a rectangular garden that he wants to cover with new topsoil. The length of the garden is four times the width. The perimeter of the garden is 300 feet. How many square feet of topsoil should Jesse purchase to cover the garden?

Our first step is to identify the **Variable**. In this case I am going to use w to identify the width of the rectangle. This problem also lends itself to a diagram. Take a look at the diagram below to see how I have identified the parts:

Next, we need to write an **E**quation based on the given information. Looking closely at the original problem, we know that the perimeter of the garden is 300 feet. Remember that the general formula for the perimeter of a rectangle is $2l + 2w = p$, where l = length, w = width, and p = perimeter.

Looking at the diagram above and the original problem, we can write the following equation:

$$2l + 2w = p$$

so $$2(4w) + 2(w) = 300$$

Next, we **S**olve the equation. We do so by combining terms and operating as we have done in previous sections:

$$2(4w) + 2(w) = 300$$

$$8w + 2w = 300$$

$$10w = 300$$

$$\frac{10w}{10} = \frac{300}{10}$$

$$w = 30$$

Now that we have solved the equation, we need to identify the **A**nswer. Recall from our previous discussion, I mentioned that the solution to the equation might not necessarily be the answer to the problem. This is an example of what I was talking about.

Reread the original problem to see what you are being asked. The problem asks: "How many square feet of topsoil should Jesse purchase to cover the garden?"

Looking back at the solution to your equation, $w = 30$, exactly what does the 30 represent? It represents the *width* of the garden. If you recall, the first step to solving this problem was to identify the variable(s). We decided to use w to represent the width of the rectangle. Now that we know that the width of the rectangle is 30 feet, we are going to need to calculate the length and then the area of the rectangle to solve the problem.

In the diagram for this problem, you will notice that the length of the rectangle was written as $4w$ to indicate that it is "four times the width." Therefore the length of the rectangle is 4 times 30, or 120 feet. Now we have both the length and the width of the rectangle.

Now we can calculate the area of the rectangle. If you recall, the area of a rectangle is the product of the length and width, in other words, $a = l \times w$.

When we plug in the values we have found, $a = l \times w$ translates to $a = 120 \times 30$, or area = 3600 square feet. *Now* we have answered the problem. Jesse would need 3600 square feet of topsoil to cover the garden.

Now that we have discussed several examples, it's time to try a few problems on your own. Remember to follow

VESA as you proceed, and make diagrams where you can. When you have finished, check your equations and your answers against those in the back of the book.

❶ When a number is multiplied by 8 and decreased by 24, the result is 240. Find the number.

❷ When a number is divided by 6 and increased by 33, the result is 73. Find the number.

❸ Twenty-six more than 9 times a number is 422. Find the number.

❹ Fifteen less than the product of a certain number and 5 is 45. What is the number?

❺ Melissa wants to carpet her living room. The length of the living room is 6 x more than 2 times the width. The perimeter of the living room is 60 feet. How many square feet of carpet will Melissa need to purchase?
(*Hint*: Use a diagram to solve this problem!)

❻ Mark and Tracy have decided to paint the exterior of their home. The exterior measurements of the house are 60 feet by 80 feet. The exterior height of the house is 10 feet. They want to purchase enough paint to cover the entire exterior with two coats. If one gallon of paint covers 60 square feet, how many gallons should they purchase?

❼ Alex wants to put ceramic tile on his kitchen floor. He wants to purchase tiles that are 8-inch squares. The length of the floor is exactly 2½ times the width. The perimeter of the floor is 70 feet. What is the total square footage of the floor and how many 8-inch tiles will he need to purchase to complete the floor?
(*Hint*: Use a diagram to solve this problem!)

Had enough algebra? Here's a quick review of the basic concepts covered in this chapter.

CHAPTER CHEAT SHEET

Integers:

Addition (same signs): Add, give same sign to answer.

Addition (different signs): Subtract, give sign of larger to answer.

Subtraction: Copy, change, change (CCC).

Multiplication: First, multiply two numbers without regard to their signs.
Then: same signs = positive answer;
different signs = negative answer.

Division: Same rules as multiplication, except divide.

Equations: Use opposite operation(s) to solve.

Problem solving: Use **VESA**.

Now that we have covered the basics of algebra, we are going to enter a new arena, that of geometry. Although high school students often wonder why, in fact it does make sense that geometry follows algebra. If you were to look closely at the content of both courses, you would find that geometry uses algebra to solve problem situations involving geometric concepts. With this in mind, we are going to proceed into geometry with the idea that algebra will remain a part of the process.

Geometry

Geometry, the study of spatial relationships, is probably one of the most fascinating aspects of mathematics. It explores how objects relate to each other
and to the space around them. Websters defines geometry
as "the branch of mathematics dealing with measurement
and properties of angles, solids, etc." Like algebra, it calls
upon your expertise with basic math skills to solve problems. Geometry uses those skills to take you one step further into the three-dimensional aspects of mathematics.

The most functional part of geometry—and the aspect
we are going to explore primarily—involves measurement
and formulas relative to perimeter, area, and volume.
These formulas make up the part of geometry for which
you are likely to find the greatest use.

Before we get into using the formulas, it is a good idea
to learn some of the basic terminology of geometry that we
are likely to use throughout our discussion of geometry.

The three most basic terms in geometry are actually
called "the three undefined terms of geometry." The rea-

son they are called this is that these three terms can't be defined precisely on the basis of simpler concepts. The terms I am speaking of are point, line, and plane. It is not difficult to provide examples or representations of these terms. For example, when we think of the term *point*, it is easiest to think of a pinpoint or a pencil point. A line is best represented by a taut length of string that extends continuously in opposite directions. A plane is best represented by a tabletop, if you think of a flat surface extending infinitely in all directions. These three basic terms form the foundation of the study of geometry. It is from these terms that the rest of geometry is derived.

There are several other basic terms that we need to discuss before we move into using formulas in geometry. Next to each term I have given an example. Hopefully this will help you better understand the term and how it will be used as we progress.

1. segment: a portion of a line with two endpoints
2. ray: a part of a line with only one endpoint
3. angle: two rays with a common endpoint
4. polygon: a closed two-dimensional figure with at least three sides
5. side: a segment that is either a part of an angle or part of a polygon
6. face: a surface of a three-dimensional object
7. edge: where two faces meet in a three-dimensional object
8. area: the surface measure of a two-dimensional object
9. volume: the capacity of a three-dimensional object
10. congruent: having the same measure

11. parallel: lines in the same plane that are equal in distance at any given point
12. perpendicular: lines that meet at 90 degree angles

With these terms in mind, the first topic we will address is perimeter. From your earlier school days, you will most likely remember perimeter as the distance around an object or shape. Let me explain further.

Perimeter

The word *perimeter* refers to the distance around a polygon. In its most simplistic form, a perimeter formula may be used to find the distance around a plot of land, for example. Let's say we wanted to know how much fence we would need to purchase to enclose a vegetable garden. We would simply measure the lengths of all the sides (assuming they are straight lines) and their sum would be the perimeter. Take a look at this example:

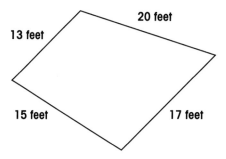

The perimeter of this quadrilateral (four-sided figure) would be determined by adding the measures of the four sides. We simply add 13 feet, 15 feet, 17 feet, and 20 feet.

The sum, 65 feet, represents the perimeter. In other words, we would need 65 feet of fencing to enclose this area for a vegetable garden.

Here's one other example before you try several on your own. Phyllis has a patio shaped as shown in the diagram below. She wants to put a hedge around this patio. How many linear (straight-line) feet of hedge would she need to enclose the patio?

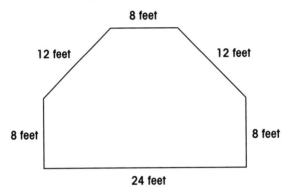

Again, you would simply add the side lengths of the figure to determine your answer. Add 8 feet, 12 feet, 8 feet, 24 feet, 8 feet, and 12 feet. The perimeter of this pentagon (five-sided polygon) is 72 feet. Therefore, Phyllis would need 72 feet of hedge to enclose the patio.

What if the longest side of the patio was up against her house? Then no hedge is needed there, and the length of that side is not included when determining the linear measure of the hedge she would need to enclose the patio. In other words, she would then need only 48 feet of hedge to complete the job.

Now try these perimeter problems and be sure to

check your answers against those in the back of the book. Also, remember to label all your answers to demonstrate that you know exactly what your answer represents.

1

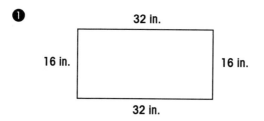

2

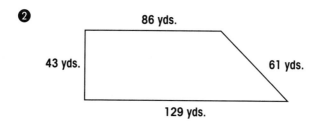

3 Melissa wants to add a wallpaper trim to her bedroom. The narrow trim would border the top and the bottom of each wall. The dimensions of her bedroom are 10 feet by 12 feet. How many linear feet of wallpaper trim will she need? The trim is packaged in 25-foot lengths. How many packages will she need to buy?

4 Alex is planning to put a new fence around his backyard. His rectangular yard is 80 feet long and 46 feet wide. One long side of the yard is up against the house, so he won't need to fence all four sides to enclose his yard. How many linear feet of fence will he need? The unit price of the fence is $24.95 per linear yard. How much will it cost Alex to fence his yard? (Remember there are 3 feet in 1 yard.)

⑤ Marty wants to put a floral border around the edge of her
garden. The dimensions of her rectangular garden are 8 feet
by 12 feet. How many linear feet will she need to cover? The
cost to put in the floral border is about $4 per linear foot.
What will the approximate cost be to enclose her garden?

The only aspect of perimeter we have not discussed in
regards to basic figures is the perimeter of a circle. The
word *perimeter* refers to the distance around a polygon. A
circle is not a polygon since it has no sides, so technically
we cannot say that a circle has a perimeter. We use the
word *circumference* when speaking about the distance
around a circle. The prefix "circum" means to go around.
Maybe this will help solidify its meaning for you.

To find the circumference of a circle, we use either of
the following formulas:

$$\textbf{Circumference} = \pi d \;\; \textbf{or} \;\; \textbf{Circumference} = 2\pi r$$

The first formula is used when we know the diameter
(d) of the circle. The second formula is used when we
know the radius (r) of the circle. The Greek letter π (pro-
nounced "pie") is used to refer to the ratio of the circumference of a circle to its diameter. You will find a more
detailed discussion of this topic in the next section, Area of
Polygons.

In the first formula, we simply multiply π (use 3.14) by
the diameter. In the second formula, we simply multiply 2
by π (use 3.14) and take that answer and multiply it by the
radius. If you realize that the diameter is the same as two
of the radii (plural form of radius), the formulas will begin

to make more sense to you. In actuality, the two formulas are really one and the same.

Here's an example to look at before you try several on your own. Find the circumference of the two circles below, noting that one shows a radius and one shows a diameter:

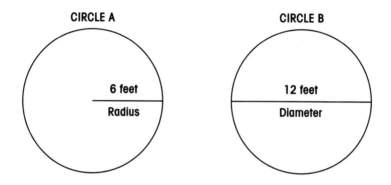

CIRCLE A

6 feet

Radius

CIRCLE B

12 feet

Diameter

To find the circumference of Circle A, we use the formula Circumference = $2\pi r$, since we know the radius of the circle. We simply multiply 2 by 3.14 by 6 feet. The result, 37.68 feet, represents the distance around the circle. By the way, when multiplying 2 by 3.14 by 6, you will probably want to multiply the 2 and the 6 first. Since the problem is all multiplication, multiply the easiest terms first to make it less difficult on yourself. Then multiply 12 by 3.14 to get your answer. In any order that you choose to multiply, you will see that the answers are exactly the same.

To find the circumference of Circle B, we use the formula Circumference = πd, since we know the diameter of the circle. We simply multiply 3.14 by 12 feet. The result, 37.68 feet, represents the distance around the circle.

Notice that both circles have exactly the same circumference. The reason for this is that the circles are congruent, since their diameters are equal. The diameter of a circle is always equal to two times its radius. This should explain it all to you.

Now, here are several circumference problems for you to solve. Remember to use 3.14 for π and to check your answers as you solve them.

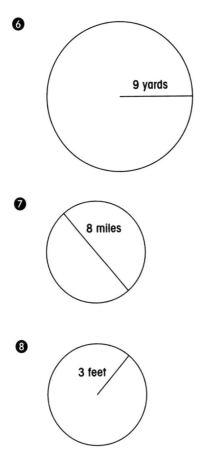

6

9 yards

7

8 miles

8

3 feet

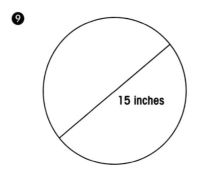

Now we have completed our discussion on perimeters. Before we move on to the topic of areas, I quickly want to clarify the difference between perimeter and area. Remember that perimeter represents the distance around an object, whereas area represents the complete surface of the object. Read on!

Area of Polygons

The term *area* refers to the surface of an object. The best explanation of area would be represented by a problem that involves, for example, installing new carpeting or tile on your floor at home. From border to border, the entire surface to be covered represents the *area* of the surface. The concept of area is useful for many things besides carpeting or tiling a floor at home. Other examples might include adding topsoil or grass to a part of your yard, painting walls in your home, and even repaving your driveway. You can begin to see from these examples that knowing how to find and work with area is a skill that is extremely practical and useful in our everyday lives.

To understand the formulas for area, it will be easier if I approach it from the aspect of *square units*. Take a look at the diagram below:

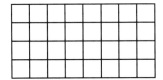

Notice that this rectangle is 8 units long and 4 units wide. Count the number of small squares in this picture. The total, 32, represents the total area of the rectangle. The formula for finding the area of a rectangle is to multiply the length by the width or the base by the height. The length, 8, multiplied by the width, 4, is 32 square units. It is appropriate to use *square* in your label since the units represent squares within the figure. Notice that this simple multiplication process accomplishes the same thing as actually counting the square units included in the figure. Granted, it could be just as easy to count in this problem, but when you have a problem with large measures, the counting process could be rather lengthy. The formula, therefore, is much easier to contend with. The first formula we will be using is:

Area of a Rectangle =

Length (Base) × Width (Height)

Take a look at the illustration below to see how the area is calculated:

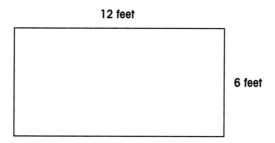

12 feet

6 feet

To find the area of the rectangle, simply multiply the length, 12 feet, by the width, 6 feet. The answer, 72 square feet, represents the square units within the rectangle.

Here's an example that uses this formula to solve: Tyler is planning to retile his kitchen floor with 12-inch square tiles. The dimensions of his kitchen are 11 feet by 8 feet. How many tiles will he need to complete the job?

To solve this problem, we simply multiply the length of the kitchen floor, 11 feet, by the width, 8 feet. Since he is planning to use 12-inch tiles (that is, each tile is 1 square foot), the number of square feet in the area, 11×8, will solve his problem. Therefore, he will need 88 tiles to retile his kitchen floor.

The formula we have been using, $A = L \times W$ or $A = B \times H$, can also be used for several other geometric figures, including squares and parallelograms. Try the problems below using this same formula and remember to check your answers against those in the back of the book as you go:

❶

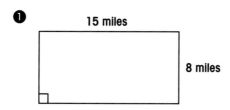

15 miles

8 miles

❷

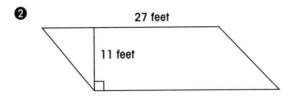

Note: The ☐ symbol represents a right angle. This is where the base of the figure and the height of the figure meet perpendicularly. To use base times height or length times width, the base and height or length and width must be perpendicular.

❸ Pedro is going to resurface his driveway. The illustration below outlines the driveway to be resurfaced. What is the total area to be resurfaced? The cost to resurface is about $22.00 per square foot. Find the approximate cost to resurface the entire driveway.

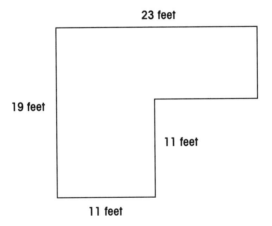

❹ Vincent has decided to paint his living room. The dimensions of the room are 22 feet by 14 feet. The walls are uniformly 8 feet high. Find the total square footage of the four walls to be painted in the living room. Each gallon of paint covers 50 square feet. How many gallons of paint should Vincent buy? The cost of paint is $12.95 per gallon. How much will it cost (not including tax) to paint Vincent's living room?

❺ Find the area of the shaded region in each of the following diagrams.

a.

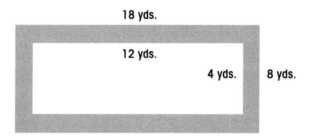

b.

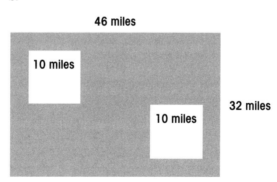

c.

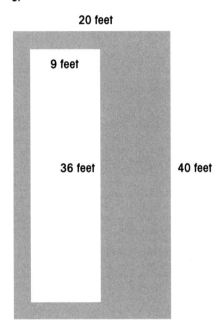

20 feet

9 feet

36 feet   40 feet

Now let's take a look at the areas of triangles and trape-zoids. Below are illustrations of a basic triangle and a trapezoid:

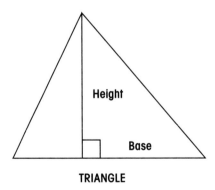

Height

Base

TRIANGLE

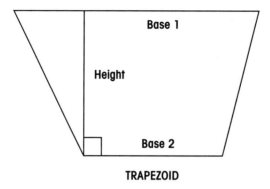

TRAPEZOID

Let's first discuss the area of a triangle. The formula looks like this:

Area = ½ × Base × Height

In other words, multiply ½ by the base and then multiply that answer by the height. Actually, since this is entirely multiplication, the order in which you multiply the factors will *not* affect your answer. You could multiply the base by the height, and then take one-half of the result. The answer will still be the same.

Let's try one example and see if it makes sense to you. Take a look at this illustration:

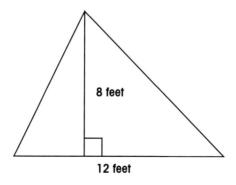

First, we need to identify the base and the height of the given triangle. In this illustration, the base is 12 feet and the height is 8 feet. Next, we substitute these values into the formula. It should look like this:

Area = ½ × 12 × 8.

I would first multiply ½ by 12, which is 6, and then multiply by 8. The result, 48, represents the area of the triangle. As with rectangles and other polygons, the area is *always* expressed in square units. Since the measurements are given in feet, the final answer is 48 square feet.

Next, let's take a look at the formula for the area of a trapezoid, which is:

Area = ½ × Height × (Base 1 + Base 2)

To calculate the area of a trapezoid, we first find the sum of Base 1 and Base 2. *Always compute inside parentheses first.* Next, multiply ½ by the height of the trapezoid. Finally, multiply the sum of the bases by ½ of the height and you will have solved the problem.

Now let's take a look at an example and see if you understand how the formula works. First you will need to identify the necessary parts to solve the problem. In other words, you will need to identify the *height* and the two *bases*.

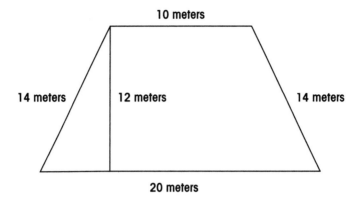

Notice in the illustration that there is more information than you need to solve the problem. The point here is to get you to separate the necessary from the unnecessary information before you solve the problem.

In this particular case, the *height* is 12 meters. We know this since the height is the length of a segment that is perpendicular to both bases of the trapezoid. The two *bases* are 10 meters and 20 meters, since these are the lengths of the two parallel sides of the trapezoid.

Now that we have determined the values we need, let's substitute these values into the formula and solve the problem. When we have substituted the values, the problem should look like this:

Area = (½) (12 meters) (10 meters + 20 meters)

Actually, the problem will be much easier to solve if you omit the labels. We'll keep in mind that all lengths are in meters, and simplify the problem to look like this:

Area = (½) (12) (10 + 20)

Notice that I used parentheses to indicate multiplication since the multiplication signs look like variables and might be confusing. Now let's finish the problem by performing the necessary operations. First, I would multiply ½ by 12. Take that answer, 6, and multiply it by the sum of 10 and 20, or 30. The final solution is 180. Since the original problem was in meters, your answer should also be labeled with the related square units. Therefore, the final answer is 180 square meters.

Here are several area problems for you to try on your own. Be careful to use only the information you need and also to label your answer. Then, check your answers against those in the back of the book as you go.

6

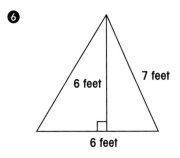

6 feet

7 feet

6 feet

7

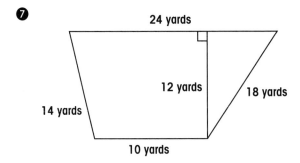

24 yards

14 yards

12 yards

18 yards

10 yards

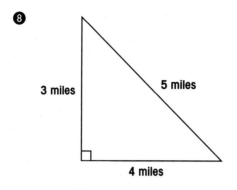

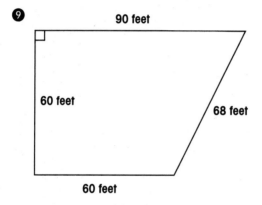

Now that we have explored the areas of basic polygons, we need to look at circles. The formula for a circle's area is very different, but if you think about the shape of the figure (compared to polygons), it begins to make sense. The formula for the area of a circle is Area $= \pi r^2$, which we read as "pi times r squared." In this formula, π refers to the ratio of the circumference (perimeter) of the circle to its diameter. In other words, if you were to divide the circumference of a circle by its diameter, you would have the value of π. In problem-solving formats, we often use 3.14

for π when solving circle problems. To calculate the area of a circle, you simply multiply π (3.14) by the radius and then by the radius again. Remember that the radius is exactly one-half of the diameter.

Here are two examples for us to discuss. Notice that one circle has a radius identified and the other has a diameter identified. We will solve both so you can see how each situation needs to be handled.

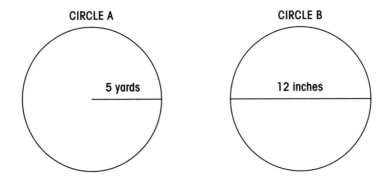

Remember that the formula for finding the area of a circle is Area $= \pi r^2$. In Circle A, we simply substitute the given value to solve. When you substitute, remember that r^2 is the same as "radius times radius." For our purposes, it is definitely easier to remember it this way. After substitution, your formula should now look like this

Area $= 3.14 \times 5$ yards $\times 5$ yards   or   Area $= (3.14)(5)(5)$

To solve, I would first multiply 5 times 5 since the problem is all multiplication and the fives are easier to multiply first. Next, multiply the answer, 25, by 3.14. Your answer, 78.5, represents the surface of the circle. But remember that your answer needs an appropriate label. In this case, your final answer is 78.5 square yards.

Does it seem strange that the circle is round, yet the area is square? Actually, the unit measures for areas (even for area of a circle) are squares, so the label is both appropriate and correct. The figure below shows you square units within a circle. I think this will help clarify my point:

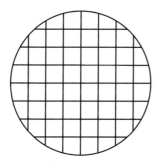

Now let's take a look at Circle B. To find the area of this circle, we use the same formula as before, only there is one further detail. We don't have the radius of the circle, we have the diameter. In Circle B, the diameter is 12 inches. If the diameter of the circle is 12 inches, then what is the length of the radius? Remember that two radii are equal to exactly one diameter. Therefore, in this problem, we will be using 6 inches as the radius (r) to solve the problem. Now that we have this information, we simply substitute into our original formula

Area = 3.14 × 6 inches × 6 inches or

Area = (3.14) (6) (6)

I would first multiply 6 by 6 since this is definitely the easy part of the problem. Take the answer, 36, and multiply it by 3.14 to arrive at the correct area. The area of Circle B would then be 113.04 square inches. Got it?

Now, it's time for you to try several of these on your own. Remember to pay particular attention to the radius and the diameter of the circles so that you use accurate information when substituting into the formula. Don't forget to check your answers against those in the back of the book as you go.

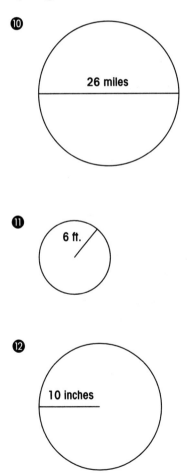

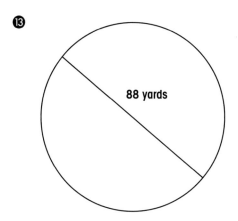

Now let's take a look at a quick review of this chapter:

CHAPTER CHEAT SHEET

Perimeter: Add up all the side lengths of the polygon.

Circumference: $C = \pi d$ or $C = 2\pi r$

Area of a Rectangle: Length times Width.

Area of a Parallelogram: Base times Height.

Area of a Triangle: ½ times Base times Height.

Area of a Trapezoid: ½ × Height × (Base 1 + Base 2).

Area of a Circle: $A = \pi r^2$

Now that we have scratched the surface with some basic geometry, let's take the next step into trigonometry. More precisely, trigonometry deals with one specific aspect of geometry: triangles. I think you'll find the topic fascinating and the applications very interesting. This is where we begin to step into what I would define as true mathematics: the logical application of problem-solving skills.

Trigonometry

The word *trigonometry* appears rather intimidating at first. In reality, the definition is rather simplistic. Mathematically speaking, trigonometry deals with triangles—primarily right triangles, but just triangles and nothing more. Hopefully, this begins to make the subject much less intimidating.

This particular aspect of math has many applications, but most frequently relates to aviation and architecture. If you fly, or ever plan on flying, you will need a basic knowledge of trigonometry to survive coursework in aviation. Angles of elevation and angles of depression are used to navigate the vehicle. Without this basic understanding, navigation would be impossible. An architect applies knowledge of trigonometry for structural integrity purposes—in other words, creating structures that are intended to remain standing. Imagine spending millions of dollars on a building only to see it fall down just before the building process is complete. Trigonometry is used to insure safe and sound building practices in terms of the actual size, shape, and design of the structure.

Before I get into the application of trigonometry, there are some basics you need to understand. Let's take a look at the *unit circle* below. This is the place where trigonometry begins. It is from here that everything related to trigonometry evolves.

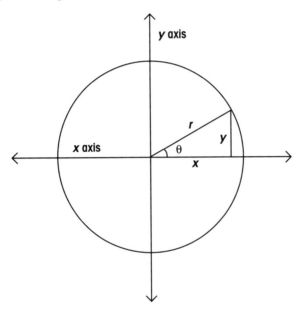

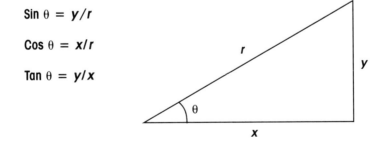

Sin θ = *y/r*

Cos θ = *x/r*

Tan θ = *y/x*

Now that you are completely confused by the preceding information, let me try to make some sense of it for you. First let's look at the illustration of the circle. Notice that the horizontal line is referred to as the x axis and the vertical line is referred to as the y axis. In the upper right-hand portion of the illustration, also known as the *first quadrant*, there is a triangle with the three sides labeled as x, y, and r. Side x refers to the side of the triangle that sits on or is parallel to the x axis (used in determining the cosine), side y refers to the side of the triangle that sits on or is parallel to the y axis (used in determining the sine), and side r refers to the side of the triangle that is also a radius of the circle. In a *unit* circle, the length of r is 1 unit, hence the term "unit circle." Now, hopefully, you see where x, y, and r come from.

Beneath the illustration of the unit circle, there is a triangle. I must impress upon you that this is a right triangle (a triangle with one 90° angle). I simply lifted this illustration from the unit circle and enlarged it so we could more easily use it for reference. Notice inside the triangle, the symbol θ is used to identify the angle. We call this "theta." The reason we use a Greek letter is so that it does not become confused with a label for one of the sides of the triangle.

Finally, we have the three basic trigonometric functions of sine, cosine, and tangent (abbreviated as Sin, Cos, and Tan). These three functions represent the most basic relationships in a triangle. Each of these functions uses the angle θ as its reference. In other words, these functions tell us how the sides of a triangle relate to each other and to the reference angle.

Note that these functions are based on the presence of one right angle in a triangle. So our discussion of trigonometry will be limited to right triangles.

Take a look at the triangle below. From the information given, I will show you exactly how the relationships work:

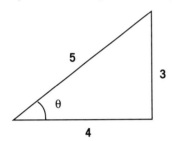

First, notice that your x value is 4, your y value is 3, and your r value is 5. This comes from the original illustration that identifies the x, y and r sides of the reference triangle. Notice that the Sin function is represented by placing the y value over the r value. In other words, in this particular example the Sin value is 3/5. What this means is that the Sin value in this triangle is represented by the fraction ⅗ or the decimal 0.6. The Cos value in this triangle is represented by the fraction ⅘ or by the decimal 0.8. The Tan value is represented by the fraction ¾ or by the decimal 0.75. You now have numeric values for the three basic trigonometric functions of this particular triangle.

Armed with this information, we can begin to apply trigonometry, but first I would like you to try a few examples to clarify your understanding of the three basic trigonometric functions:

Find the fractional and decimal value for each of the following (remember to reduce all fractions to lowest terms):

Triangle A:

1 Sin θ =

2 Cos θ =

3 Tan θ =

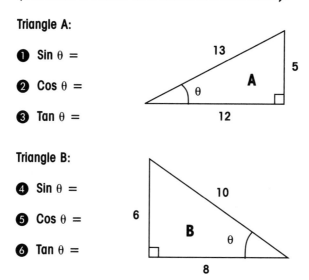

Triangle B:

4 Sin θ =

5 Cos θ =

6 Tan θ =

Now that you have a basic understanding of the three basic trigonometric functions, let's put them to use. Look back at Triangle A in the last illustration. Notice that Sin θ was 5/13. When we divide 5 by 13, the result is 0.3846 to the nearest ten-thousandth. If we were to enter the value of 0.3846 into a scientific calculator and press the keys 2nd or INV and Sin in that order, the calculator would then tell us the measure, in degrees, of the angle θ. In this case, that is about 22.5°. Now that you know that θ is 22.5°, can you determine the other two angles in this triangle? Well, we know that one of the angles is 90° since this is a right triangle. We also know that the sum of the measures of the angles in a triangle is 180°. So by subtraction, we can determine the value, in degrees, of the third angle. That would be 67.5°.

To work comfortably with trigonometry, one last basic concept you will need is the Pythagorean Theorem. You really don't need to remember the name; however, the principle is very important. You might recall that the scarecrow in *The Wizard of Oz*, upon receiving his "brain," recites the Pythagorean Theorem. There's a bit of trivia for you. He states: "The sum of the squares of the legs in a right triangle is equal to the square of the hypotenuse in that same triangle."

Now, in English, here's how it works The two short sides in a right triangle are called the legs. The long side (directly opposite the right angle) is called the hypotenuse. If you take the measures of the legs in the right triangle, square each one separately and add the results together, their sum will equal the square of the measure of the hypotenuse in the same right triangle.

Pythagorean Theorem

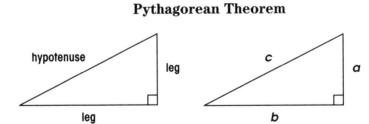

$$a^2 + b^2 = c^2$$

Here's an example of the Pythagorean Theorem for you to see. After demonstrating, I will give you several to try. They are really quite elementary. Find the hypotenuse of a right triangle if the legs are 6 cm and 8 cm long. Let's plug the given lengths into the formula and go from there. Remember that a and b are the legs and c is the hypotenuse. Therefore $6^2 + 8^2 = c^2$. We know that $6^2 = 36$ and $8^2 = 64$ and their sum is 100. We now ask ourselves what number, multiplied by itself, gives us 100. The answer is obviously 10; therefore, the hypotenuse of the triangle is 10 cm.

Now try these on your own. Round your answers to the nearest tenth, if necessary.

7 $a = 5,$ $b = 12,$ $c = $ _____

8 $a = 9,$ $b = 12,$ $c = $ _____

9 $a = 7,$ $b = $ _____, $c = 11$

10 $a = $ _____, $b = 14,$ $c = 20$

In terms of aviation and architecture, you should begin to see how this information could be useful. Now here's a problem I am going to present *and* solve for you so you can begin to see the applications of trigonometry at work.

Look at the illustration below:

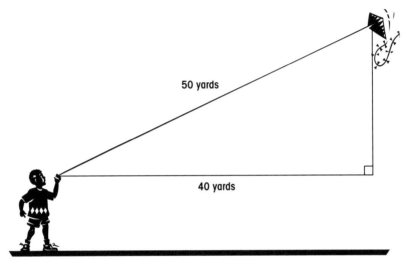

Christopher is flying his kite in the backyard this after-
noon. He has only 50 yards of twine and has the kite fully
extended. He is standing exactly 40 yards from a point on
the ground that is directly below the kite. How high is the
kite off the ground?

To solve this, we will need to use the Pythagorean Theorem. Using the formula $a^2 + b^2 = c^2$, we plug in the necessary information. We know that $b = 40$ and $c = 50$, so
we now have a problem that should proceed this way:

$$a^2 + b^2 = c^2$$

$$a^2 + 40^2 = 50^2$$

$$a^2 + 1600 = 2500$$

$$a^2 = 900$$

$$a = 30$$

Therefore, the kite is 30 yards off the ground.

Now here are several problems for you to try using trigonometry and its applications:

⓫ Chris is standing 60 feet away from a tree. From where he is standing to the very top of the tree is 100 feet. What is the height of the tree?

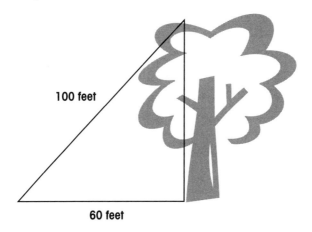

100 feet

60 feet

⓬ Joe is standing on the ground looking up at an airplane. The plane is 5000 feet off the ground. He is standing 3000 feet away from a point on the ground that is directly below the plane. What is the approximate distance between Joe and the airplane?

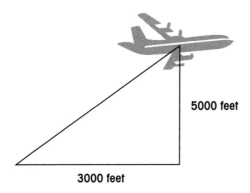

5000 feet

3000 feet

In case you haven't noticed, we used the Pythagorean Theorem to solve both of the previous problems. Now here are several that utilize your knowledge of the three basic trigonometric functions.

⑬ A helicopter is hovering at 1500 feet above a helipad. A team of doctors is standing ready to unload an emergency patient from the helicopter. The angle of elevation from the doctors to the helicopter is 40°. Which function—Sin, Cos, or Tan— would help you determine how far the doctors are from the spot on the helipad where the helicopter will land?

⑭ An airplane is approaching its landing at the airport. The plane is about 1600 yards from the runway and the angle of depression (same as angle of elevation from the ground to the plane) is 30°. Which function—Sin, Cos, or Tan—would you use to determine how high off the ground the airplane currently is?

⑮ The angle of elevation to the top of a skyscraper from a ground-level point 200 feet away from the base of the building is 65°. Which function would you use to determine how tall the building is?

Here you will find several useful bits of information from this chapter on trigonometry to refer to as needed.

CHAPTER CHEAT SHEET

1. Sin $\theta = y/r$

2. Cos $\theta = x/r$

3. Tan $\theta = y/x$

4. Pythagorean Theorem:
$$a^2 + b^2 = c^2$$

Now that we have looked into one of the more applicable aspects of math, we are going to switch gears ever so slightly and look at a more entertaining side of math. In contrast to the logical study of shapes that comprises the subject of geometry, optical illusions take everything you learned about spatial relationships and completely destroy any logic connected to them—but it sure is fun looking at the images. So move on to the next chapter and enjoy!

The Eyes Have It

Optical Illusions

Optical illusions have always been a fun and fascinating side of mathematics. The expression "things are not always as they appear" has never been more true than in optical illusions. With most optical illusions, the longer you look, the more the image changes. Think about today's newest visual treats. The new three-dimensional images now available on posters and calendars as well as in books take a little *getting used to*—but once you have learned the trick, they're fun, they're interesting, and they're purely mathematical!

Now most people would look at these and ask, "What do optical illusions have to do with math?" Remember that geometry is the exploration of spatial relationships. It is a very concrete and very exacting field of math. Optical illusions are also an exploration of spatial relationships; however, the tables are now turned—nothing is the way it appears, nothing is very exact. All of a sudden, there are visual contradictions when geometry was visually correct.

Yes, it is confusing, but it is also fun at the same time. Here we can take a humorous look, if you will, at the contradictions of geometry, otherwise known as *optical illusions.*

Look at the image below. You'll notice that the longer you look, the more the image changes. Give yourself at least 20 to 30 seconds to really look. Try to stay focused on the black box in the center and watch what happens.

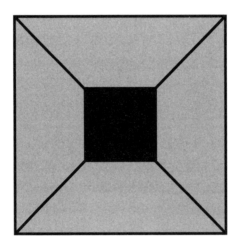

If you focus on the black box in the center, it should appear in the background and then the foreground and then back again. It should keep changing the longer you look. Now look at the same illustration, again for at least 20 to 30 seconds, with a white box in the center and see if you notice anything different.

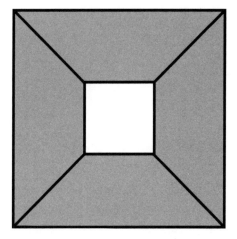

Actually, if you were to look long enough the same thing should happen. The white center box should appear to be alternately in the background and then in the foreground. It will keep switching positions the longer you look.

Now take a look at the next combination of the same images. What do you see going on now?

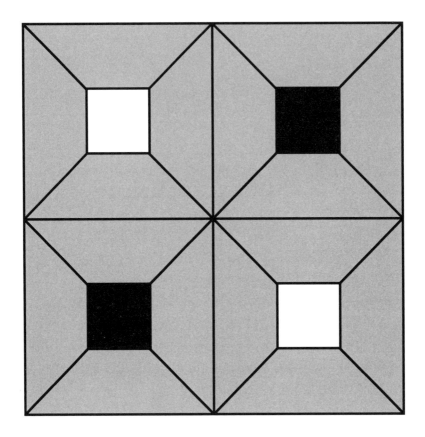

Once again, look at the image for at least 20 to 30 seconds and you should notice the images all changing. That is, the center boxes will keep alternating between background and foreground. You might want to try focusing on one center box for a while and then focus on a different center box and see what happens. As a result, the center boxes again appear to move between background and foreground. The fact that your eyes are solely responsible for the apparent changes in the images makes this an optical illusion.

Now look at a combination of circles that have a similar spatial relationship. What do you see happening here?

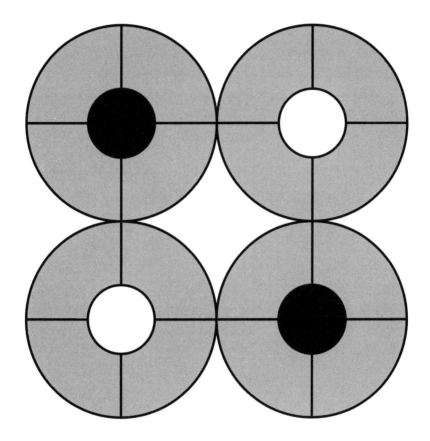

What you should notice is the same effect that took place with the squares. The center images, in this case circles, seem to shift from background to foreground and back again.

Now here's another image that is likely to play games with your eyes. Look at the image, again, for at least 20 to 30 seconds and see what happens.

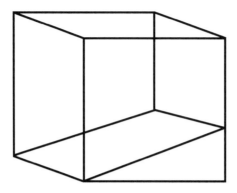

The longer you watch the image, the more frequently the positioning of the image changes. The two images we are specifically looking for have (a) the upper left corner in the back and (b) the upper left corner in the front of the picture. If you don't see it immediately, be patient, the images will present themselves for you.

Now here's one final image to contemplate. Again, focus on the image for a minimum of 20 to 30 seconds.

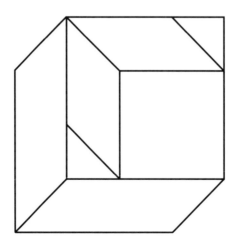

The two boxes in this illustration seem to contradict each other. The smaller, inside box technically cannot be situated the way it is and yet touch the two adjacent walls of the larger box. This is the optical illusion. Your eyes will first focus on one box and then the other, but your eyes will also tell you that they cannot face the directions they appear to face and still coincide in the same illustration.

Now that we have explored the concept of optical illusions, we are going to move on to puzzles. Riddles, tricks, and puzzles have long entertained people of all ages. They can be extremely simple or very complex, or moderately challenging. Any way you look at them, puzzles are entertaining, fun, and purely mathematical.

Brain Teasers and Number Tricks

Now we have arrived at one of my favorite parts of the book. I thoroughly enjoy problems that challenge the mind—problems that can take several minutes to solve if you're lucky, or several hours if you are not. Sometimes called *brain teasers,* they usually do what they set out to do, namely, tease the brain.

Brain teasers, number tricks, and problem solving have long been the most stimulating and, in my estimation, the most fun part of math. I have selected for you some of the most thought-provoking, sometimes frustrating problems strictly for your enjoyment.

These problems will ask you to call upon your basic math skills and even more. With each situation comes a brand new experience. Be sure you read each problem very carefully along with the directions before you begin, and remember that, if all else fails, the answers are always in the back of the book. Have fun!

❶ There are 12 green socks and 12 blue socks in a drawer. Find the least number of socks you would have to pull to make one matched pair.

❷ How many years have to pass before all calendars would be used at least once, including those for leap years?

❸ How many coin combinations can you devise that total exactly one dollar without using more than ten coins? You may use less than ten coins, but the value must be exactly $1.00.

❹ Which prize would you rather have: one million dollars, or a prize that starts with one penny and doubles each day for exactly one month with the coin value added in each day?

❺ Can you predict the next two problems and their results based on the given information?

$$1 \times 1 = 1$$
$$11 \times 11 = 121$$
$$111 \times 111 = 12321$$
$$?$$
$$?$$

6 Can you draw the figure below with one continuous line?
You may *not* lift your pencil off the paper once you have
begun. You may *not* go over the same line twice.

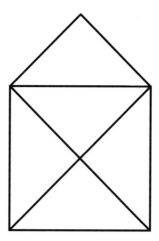

7 Using one continuous line as in the previous problem, trace
this figure without going over the same line twice.

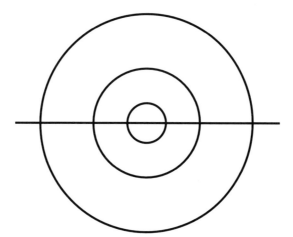

8 Can you move three sticks to make three squares?
Remember that the definition of a square is a polygon with
four equal sides.

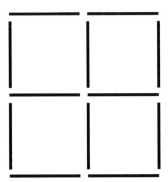

9 Can you add three lines to this number to form a word that
describes a tramp?

10 The diagram below is the frame for a *magic square.* The magic lies in the fact that when you have filled in each box with a number from one through nine (using each number only once), the sum of three numbers in any direction will be exactly the same. In other words, when you add up or down, across, or diagonally, the sum is exactly the same. Can you fill in the boxes to make this a magic square?

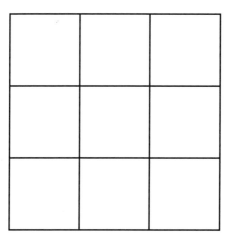

11 Using six sticks, can you make exactly four equilateral triangles? Remember that an equilateral triangle has three equal sides.

⑫ A palindrome is a word or number that reads the same backward as it does forward. For example, the word *pup* is a palindrome. How many four-digit palindromes can you find?

⑬ Can you remove six lines and leave "ten" in the illustration below?

⑭ How many triangles can you find in the illustration below?

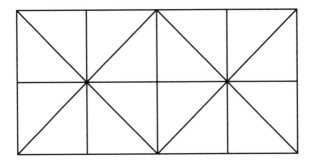

⑮ A piece of string is 30 inches long. If you wanted to cut it into 1-inch pieces with scissors, what is the least number of cuts necessary?

⑯ On the table there is a bowl with 15 apples in it. How many apples would you have if you took 5 apples?

Although puzzles and brain teasers can be a lot of fun, so can calculators. Most people are totally unaware of the possibilities calculators have. The final chapter will open your eyes to the possibilities that calculators possess.

Calculator Tricks and Games

Since the arrival of the calculator, we have been blessed with this major *little* invention that has made life so much easier for us all. I remember studying algebra and trigonometry in high school in the late sixties, when we had to learn to use a slide rule. It was *not* fun! Actually, I scarcely remember how to use one anymore, since the calculator has become the principal player today.

Calculators have made math so much easier and so much more fun. In addition to solving basic mathematical operations, calculators are capable of so much more. First of all, calculators usually have memories, which is more than I can say for myself. Many simple, inexpensive calculators can also work with square roots, percents, and even exponents. The time saved by this little gadget is truly amazing.

More advanced calculators, including scientific and graphing calculators, perform advanced mathematical functions at breakneck speed and with pinpoint accuracy that boggle the mind. Today, the graphing calculator is the epitome of current technology: It can take an equation and graph it (yes, it actually draws the graph for you!) and define its boundaries and limitations. It is truly a miraculous invention. Since the introduction of the computer, the technology available to math has advanced to incredibly high levels.

Now that I have brought you up to date on the uses of calculators, I want to show you how much fun you can have with them. I also want to show you how to make calculators more useful for yourself.

Most calculators have a keyboard that is similar to the illustration below. I have taken the liberty to label the keys so that you will be able to follow along as we progress through this chapter. Please note that your calculator may have a slightly different arrangement of keys. If so, you may wish to refer to this illustration from time to time, for it is the premise upon which this chapter is based.

Let's begin with the basic functions of the calculator. Listed below you will find the basic keys on the face of the calculator and the purpose or function of each key. As we progress through the chapter, I will explain how the keys are used in actual situations.

RCM	recall information stored in the memory
M−	delete information from the memory
M+	add information to the memory
÷	perform division
ON	turns the calculator on
×	perform multiplication

OFF turns the calculator off
  −   perform subtraction
CE clear the most current entry
  √   find a square root
  %   find percents
  +   perform addition
  =   exhibit the result of operations
  .   a decimal point

The rest of the keys on the face of the calculator are numeric and represent the single-digit values indicated. For our discussion, I'd like to begin with the memory functions of the calculator. First, it is important to understand that values will remain in the memory of the calculator until such time as you choose to delete them. Few calculators will automatically delete the memory when you turn the calculator off.

Before we get into puzzles and games to explore with your calculator, I'd like to spend a little time on the less understood functions of the calculator so you can maximize your calculator's use in your personal and business life.

The memory keys are usually the least understood and the least used keys on the calculator. Let's say you wanted to solve a multistep problem. For example, try solving this problem $(525 \times 12) + (225 \times 15)$. Before you begin, you want to be sure that the memory of the calculator is empty. Press RCM (recall memory) to see if there are any values. If a number other than zero appears on the display, you will want to erase it. To do this, simply press M– or the RCM button (it depends on the calculator). The memory should clear if you press the button twice. Now you are ready to proceed with the problem. On your calculator, first multiply 525 by 12. After you press the equal button, your answer, 6300, can be stored in the memory by pressing the M+ button; then you can bring up this value again after you have finished the second step of the problem. In other words, after you press the = key, press the M+ button to store the answer in the calculator memory.

Now you are ready to proceed with the second half of the problem. Multiply 225 by 15. Press the = key to arrive at the answer of 3375 and then press the M+ button to recall the value stored. Press the + key and your calculator will add the two figures. You should have a total of 9675.

Now try several on your own and remember to check your answers in the back of the book.

❶ (444 × 16) + (276 × 18)

❷ (864 ÷ 9) + (315 × 47)

❸ (575 × 35) − (846 ÷ 6)

❹ (813 × 29) − (656 × 33)

❺ (909 ÷ 9) + (632 × 71) − (716 × 24)

Now that you have an idea how the memory keys operate, let's try several activities that are intended to be more fun for you. First, here's a cross-number puzzle; it works just like a crossword puzzle but uses numbers.

ACROSS

1. 36 × 23

3. 5^3

4. $3^2 × 5$

DOWN

2. 20,375 ÷ 25

To solve this puzzle, simply solve the problems in the *Across* and *Down* columns and place the answers into the puzzle. Remember there can be only one digit in each unshaded box. Your finished puzzle should look like this:

8[1]	2	8[2]		
		1[3]	2	5
	4[4]	5		

Now, here's a cross-number puzzle for you to try on your own. This puzzle will be relatively easy, but you will find that using your calculator will make it even simpler for you:

ACROSS

3. 265×25

6. 98×88

7. $5^3 \times 2^2$

8. 116×3

DOWN

1. $76{,}896 \div 8$

2. $299{,}152 \div 56$

4. $2^2 \times (14 \div 2)$

5. 400×14

7. 29×2^1

After you have finished, compare your results to the completed puzzle in the back of the book. Now we're going to try one that is a little more difficult. Just remember that there can be only one digit in each unshaded box. The rest is easy! And don't forget to use your calculator.

ACROSS

1. $2^3 \times 811$

4. 2×49

6. $3 \times 5 \times 491$

9. $19,320 \div 805$

10. Next palindrome after 4994

11. $18 + 52 - 22$

DOWN

2. $6N - 94 = 158, N = ?$

3. 633 is 75% of ?

4. $1812 \times \frac{1}{2}$

5. $67 \times 3 \times 4$

7. $5190 \div 15$

8. 17×2^2

ACROSS

13. 7629 − 7587

15. 2^6

16. $\dfrac{4 \times 4 \times 7}{2}$

18. 1372 ÷ 49

20. 3024 ÷ 7 ÷ 8

22. Four more than two times three times five

23. 2 cubed times 3 squared

24. 20% of 2510

26. $(12 \times 18) + (2^2 \times 5 \times 10^2)$

29. Palindrome just before 585

30. $2^4 \times 2^5$

32. 1936 ÷ 44

33. $(48 \times 15) − (50 \times 8)$

34. $36 + [12 \times (36 + 14)]$

35. $\sqrt{1296}$

36. $2^3 \times 6^2$

37. 25 × 29

38. 25% of 5100

40. 323 is 50% of ?

DOWN

12. $(45 \times 25) − (5000 \div 10)$

14. $\sqrt{625}$

16. 33 ⅓% of 162

17. 3 × 11 × 25

19. $(432 \times 881) +$ $(42{,}503 \times 10)$

21. ⅕ × 210

22. 2 × 3 × 2 × 3

23. $(858 \times 496) + 345{,}274$

25. 35 ×61

27. 608 is 25% of ?

28. 801 + 666

29. ⅔ of 7929

31. 2288 ÷ 88

33. $10N − 155 = 165, N =?$

37. 40% of 1925

38. $\sqrt{121}$

39. 69,852 − 69,797

41. 25^2

43. 20% of 430

45. 21 is ½ of ?

clues continue on next page

ACROSS

42. $3N - 48 = 168$, $N =$?

43. $2916 \div 36$

44. $(36 \times 20) - (111 \times 6)$

46. $1210 \div 55$

47. What is 80% of 120?

48. ⅔ of 72

50. 840×0.025

52. $98 - 7^2$

53. $N - 458 = 767$, $N =$?

54. 0.5×32

56. $40,400 \div 20$

57. $2^2 \times 11$

58. $100 \times 19 \times 5$

DOWN

47. $(16 \times 26) + 24^2$

48. $\dfrac{N}{4} - 63 = 43$, $N =$?

49. $29,664 \div 36$

51. $23 \times (38 - 33)$

52. $2^3 \times 5$

55. 120 is 200% of ?

Through all these problems and puzzles, I hope to have enlightened you, at least a little, to the endless possibilities of mathematics. The joys and frustrations can be equaled only by the sheer satisfaction of having solved that difficult problem we never thought we would be able to do. If I have tickled your appetite for new possibilities, then I have accomplished my task.

Thank you for allowing me to play games with you and for giving me the opportunity to awaken these new possibilities in your own mind. So often, it takes someone else to open our eyes to other possibilities that eventually lead us to new horizons. If I have even come close to reaching this goal with you, then my job is done.

Just remember, there is no problem you cannot solve, no situation you cannot get out of, as long as you rely on your own abilities in math.

There is no reason to be *afraid* of math—it's just a bunch of numbers!

Answer Key

Chapter 1: Whole Numbers

Patterns (p. 9)

❶ 11, 16, 22 *(add 1, add 2, add 3, etc.)*

❷ 85, 79, 72 *(subtract 1, subtract 2, etc.)*

❸ 25, 36, 49 *(perfect squares)*

❹ 345, 405, 455 *(add 100, add 90, etc.)*

❺ 77, 157, 317 *(multiply by 2, then add 3)*

❻ 125, 216, 343 *(perfect cubes)*

❼ 3, 6, 9 *(add 3)*

❽ 16, −32, 64 *(multiply by negative 2)*

❾ 16, 8, 4 *(divide by 2)*

❿ 11, 22, 23 *(add 1, multiply by 2, repeat)*

Addition (pp. 10–16)

❶	80		❷	130
❸	90		❹	60
❺	76		❻	103
❼	77		❽	101
❾	586		❿	786
⓫	1280		⓬	1290
⓭	112,220		⓮	172,120
⓯	1,422,120		⓰	130,443
⓱	140,945		⓲	1,291,200
⓳	172,221		⓴	260,220
㉑	1,529,220			

Subtraction (p. 17)

❶	15,707		❷	306,229
❸	4,513,073			

Multiplication (pp. 18–22)

❶	Given		❷	60
❸	75		❹	72
❺	88		❻	100
❼	90		❽	250

⑨ 132

⑩ 32,000

⑪ 56,000

⑫ 240,000

⑬ 4,800,000

⑭ 4,800,000

⑮ 7,500,000

⑯ 75,000,000

⑰ 392

⑱ 1960

⑲ 24,984

⑳ 44,634

㉑ 220,332

㉒ 134,708

㉓ 4,371,466

㉔ 21,791,289

Puzzles (p. 24)

❶ $1 + 11/1$

❷ $2 \times 2 \times 2 + 2$

❸ $333/3$

❹ $4 \times (4/4) + 4$

❺ $5 \times 5 + 55$

❻ $(66/6) + 6$

❼ $7(7 - 7) + 7 \times 7$

❽ $88/88$

❾ $9 + 9 \times (9/9)$

Twos (p. 25)

$2 \times (2 - 2) \times 2 = 0$

$2 \times 2 + (2/2) = 5$

$(2 \times 2) \div (2 \times 2) = 1$

$2 \times 2 \times 2 - 2 = 6$

$(2/2) + (2/2) = 2$

$2 \times 2 \times 2 + 2 = 10$

$2 \times 2 - (2/2) = 3$

$(2 \times 2 + 2) \times 2 = 12$

$2 \times 2 + 2 - 2 = 4$

Threes (p. 25)

$33/33 = 1$ $3 + 3 + (3/3) = 7$

$3 \times 3 - 3 - 3 = 3$ $3 \times 3 - (3/3) = 8$

$(3 \times 3 + 3)/3 = 4$ $3 \times 3 \times (3/3) = 9$

$3 + 3 - (3/3) = 5$ $3 \times 3 + (3/3) = 10$ or

$3 + 3 + (3-3) = 6$ $(33 - 3)/3 = 10$

Star Puzzle (p. 26)

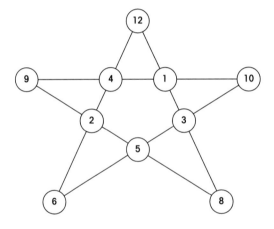

Chapter 2: Decimals and Fractions

Patterns (pp. 31–32)

❶ 0.0001, 0.00001, 0.000001

❷ 4.0004, 5.00005, 6.000006

❸ 6.6, 5.5, 4.4

❹ 444.444, 33.33, 2.2

❺ 8.08, 4.04, 2.02

❻ $\dfrac{1}{5}$, $\dfrac{1}{6}$, $\dfrac{1}{7}$

❼ $\dfrac{4}{5}$, $\dfrac{5}{4}$, $\dfrac{6}{3}$

❽ $\dfrac{8}{4}$, $\dfrac{16}{2}$, $\dfrac{32}{1}$

❾ $\dfrac{1}{2}$, $\dfrac{3}{8}$, $\dfrac{1}{4}$

❿ $\dfrac{4}{5}$, $\dfrac{5}{6}$, $\dfrac{6}{7}$

Conversions (pp. 33–35)

❶ 0.15

❷ 0.46

❸ 0.7

❹ 0.75

❺ *a.* 60¢　*b.* 24¢　*c.* 36¢

❻ 0.875

❼ $0.\overline{4}$

❽ $0.\overline{3}$

❾ $0.91\overline{6}$

❿ 34¢

answers continue on next page

⑪ $\dfrac{4}{100}$ ⑫ $\dfrac{25}{10,000}$

⑬ $\dfrac{225}{1000}$ ⑭ $\dfrac{8}{10,000}$

⑮ 0.64

Add/Subtract Decimals (pp. 37–38)

❶ 31.628   ❷ 242.312

❸ 421.567   ❹ 882.617

❺ 15.999 + 5.1   ❻ 272.87

❼ 666.903   ❽ 455.187

❾ 621.798   ❿ $24.55

Add/Subtract Fractions (pp. 42–43)

❶ $\dfrac{1}{3}$ ❷ $\dfrac{1}{4}$

❸ $\dfrac{5}{7}$ ❹ $\dfrac{5}{8}$

❺ $\dfrac{18}{15}$ or $1\dfrac{1}{5}$ ❻ $\dfrac{9}{40}$

❼ $\dfrac{24}{24}$ or 1   ❽ $\dfrac{8}{120}$ or $\dfrac{1}{15}$

❾ Yes, you will have 6 $\frac{1}{10}$ lbs.

Multiplying Decimals (pp. 45–46)

1 105.168

2 372.38

3 226.25

4 165.319

5 $3.92

6 8415.16

7 18.4464

8 469,123

9 0.252

10 $24.50

Multiplying Fractions (pp. 48–49)

1 $\dfrac{9}{20}$

2 $\dfrac{4}{21}$

3 $\dfrac{1}{3}$

4 $\dfrac{5}{8}$

5 $\dfrac{3}{10}$, $\dfrac{1}{2}$

Dividing Decimals (pp. 50–53)

1 23.6

2 18.9

3 24.4

4 45.66

5 $12.50

6 8.7

7 11.6

8 12.2

9 46.5

10 3320.50 ÷ 4 = 830.125. This is less than the monthly expenditure per person. The family will not be able to maintain their monthly budget.

Dividing Fractions (p. 54)

❶ $2\dfrac{2}{9}$

❷ $\dfrac{2}{3}$

❸ $\dfrac{3}{4}$

❹ $1\dfrac{1}{8}$

❺ 3

Chapter 3: Percents

Conversions (pp. 60–65)

❶	0.48	❷	0.152
❸	5.00	❹	0.2666
❺	0.0875	❻	¼
❼	⅗	❽	³⁹⁄₁₀₀
❾	³⁄₅₀	❿	¼
⓫	1 ½	⓬	3
⓭	4 ⅗	⓮	7 ¼
⓯	⁵⁄₂ or 2 ½	⓰	¹⁄₅₀₀
⓱	³⁄₄₀₀	⓲	¹⁄₂₀₀₀
⓳	¹⁄₁₆₀	⓴	¹⁄₁₂₅
㉑	66%	㉒	80%
㉓	62.5%	㉔	40%

㉕ 55%   ㉖ 75%

㉗ 40%   ㉘ 70%

㉙ 87.5%   ㉚ 25%

Percent Problems (p. 69)

❶ 180   ❷ 33 ⅓%

❸ 200   ❹ 2400

❺ 1232   ❻ 20%

❼ 245   ❽ 657

❾ 360   ❿ 60 tiles

Discounts (pp. 72–73)

❶ $100.00, $400.00   ❷ $40.00, $80.00

❸ $12.50, $12.50   ❹ $500.00, $1500.00

❺ $300.00, $450.00   ❻ $2.00, $18.00

❼ $12.00, $28.00   ❽ $30.00, $20.00

❾ $280.00, $70.00   ❿ $13,666.67

Increase & Decrease (p. 76)

❶ 40% decrease   ❷ 66⅔% increase

❸ 100% increase   ❹ 60% increase

❺ 66⅔% increase   ❻ 137½%

❼ 67%

Simple Interest (p. 79)

❶ $48   ❷ $540

❸ $130   ❹ $138.28

❺ $90.30

Compound Interest (pp. 84–85)

❶ $5000 [1 + (0.01 × 6)/1]^{(10 × 1)}$; $8954.24

❷ $4000 [1 + (0.01 × 8/2)]^{(5 × 2)}$; $5920.98

❸ $8000 [1 + (0.01 × 7.5/4)]^{(3 × 4)}$; $12,443.63

❹ $10000 [1 + (0.01 × 5.75/1)]^{(6 × 1)}$; $13,985.64

❺ $6000 = P[1 + (0.01 × 8/4)]^{(10 × 4)}$; $2717.34

Chapter 4: Algebra

Operations with Integers (pp. 89–95)

❶ +108   ❷ −200

❸ +360   ❹ −90

❺ 0   ❻ −120

❼ +48   ❽ +36

❾ 0   ❿ +2200

⓫ +22   ⓬ −7

⓭ +5   ⓮ −3

⑮ $+11$ ⑯ -20

⑰ -5 ⑱ $+28$

⑲ -61 ⑳ $+61$

㉑ $+103$ ㉒ -44

㉓ -6 ㉔ $+4$

㉕ -15 ㉖ $+19$

㉗ $+20$ ㉘ $+21$

㉙ -87 ㉚ $+35$

㉛ $+33$ ㉜ $+142$

㉝ $+12$ ㉞ $+27$

㉟ -93 ㊱ $+80$

㊲ -38 ㊳ -141

㊴ $+87$ ㊵ -2

㊶ $+48$ ㊷ -68

㊸ $+71$ ㊹ -45

㊺ $+13$ ㊻ -139

㊼ $+26$

Solving Equations (p. 98–104)

❶ $c = 16$ ❷ $b = 89$

❸ $n = -9$ ❹ $f = -8$

answers continue on next page

⑤ $z = -90$ **⑥** $n = 12$

⑦ $y = 144$ **⑧** $f = 13$

⑨ $z = 555$ **⑩** $c = 12.5$ or $12\frac{1}{2}$

⑪ $t = 10$ **⑫** $k = 14$

⑬ $r = 11$ **⑭** $g = 15$

⑮ $j = 11$

Problem Solving (p. 110)

❶ $8n - 24 = 240$, $n = 33$

❷ $n/6 + 33 = 73$, $n = 240$

❸ $26 + 9n = 422$, $n = 44$

❹ $5n - 15 = 45$, $n = 12$

❺ $(2w + 6) + (w) + (2w + 6) + (w) = 60$,
$w = 8$, $l = 2w + 6 = 22$, $(l)(w) = 176$ square feet

❻ $(60)(10) + (60)(10) + (80)(10) + (80)(10) = $
2800 square feet, $2800 \div 60 = 46.67$,
46.67 (gallons for one coat) $\times 2$ (coats) $= 93.33$,
or 94 gallons

❼ $(2.5w) + (2.5w) + (w) + (w) = 70$,
$w = 10$, $l = 25$,
Area $= l \times w = 10 \times 25 = 250$ square feet,
$250 \times 144 = 36{,}000$ square inches
$36{,}000 \div 64$ (8-inch square tiles) $= 562.5$ or 563 tiles

Chapter 5: Geometry

Perimeter (p. 117–121)

1. 96 inches
2. 319 yards
3. 88 linear feet, 4 packages
4. 172 linear feet, $1430.47
5. 40 feet, $160
6. 56.52 yards
7. 25.12 miles
8. 18.84 feet
9. 47.1 inches

Area (pp. 123–135)

1. 120 square miles
2. 297 square feet
3. 305 square feet, $6710
4. 576 square feet, 12 gallons, $155.40
5. *a.* 96 square yards;
   b. 1272 square miles;
   c. 476 square feet
6. 18 square feet
7. 204 square yards
8. 6 square miles
9. 4500 square feet
10. 530.66 square miles
11. 113.04 square feet
12. 314 square inches
13. 6079.04 square yards

Chapter 6: Trigonometry

(pp.141–146)

❶ $5/13$, 0.3846   ❷ $12/13$, 0.9231

❸ $5/12$, 0.4167   ❹ $3/5$, 0.6

❺ $4/5$, 0.8   ❻ $3/4$, 0.75

❼ 13   ❽ 15

❾ 8.5   ❿ 14.3

⓫ 80 feet   ⓬ 5831 feet

⓭ Tangent   ⓮ Sine

⓯ Tangent

Chapter 8: Brain Teasers & Number Tricks

(pp. 158–162)

❶ 13 socks

❷ 28 years

❸ There are over 26 possible combinations.

❹ One penny doubled each day becomes the greater prize.

❺ $1111 \times 1111 = 1234321$
$11111 \times 11111 = 123454321$

6 Yes, it can be done as follows:

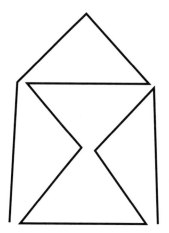

7

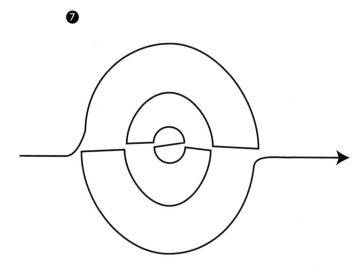

8

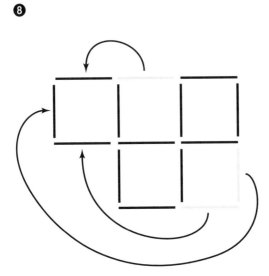

9

10 One possible arrangement:

4	9	2
3	5	7
8	1	6

⓫ The solution is a three-dimensional figure called a regular tetrahedrom. Viewed from above, the sticks would look like this:

⓬ There are 90 four-digit palindromes. The first (and last) digit can be chosen from 1–9. The second (and third) digit can be 0–9.

⓭ Remove the six sticks shown here as gray lines and you will be left with the word "TEN."

⓮ There are 36 triangles in this illustration when triangles of all possible sizes are taken into account.

⓯ It would take 29 cuts. The last 2 inches are divided by one cut.

⓰ You would have 5 apples if you *took* 5 apples.

Chapter 9: Calculator Tricks and Games

(p. 169)

❶ 12,072   ❷ 14,901

❸ 19,984   ❹ 1929

❺ 27,789

(p. 171)

9¹					5²
6³	6	2⁴	5⁵		3
1		8⁶	6	2	4
2			0		2
		5⁷	0	0	
3⁸	4	8			

(p. 172)

6[1]	4[2]	8[3]	8		9[4]	8[5]		7[6]	3[7]	6[8]	5
	2[9]	4		5[10]	0	0	5		4[11]	8	
6[12]		4[13]	2[14]		6[15]	4		5[16]	6		8[17]
2[18]	8[19]		5[20]	4[21]			3[22]	4		7[23]	2
5[24]	0	2[25]		2[26]	2[27]	1[28]	6		5[29]	7	5
	5[30]	1	2[31]		4[32]	4		3[33]	2	0	
	6[34]	3	6		3[35]	6		2[36]	8	8	
7[37]	2	5		1[38]	2	7	5[39]		6[40]	4	6[41]
7[42]	2		8[43]	1			5[44]	4[45]		2[46]	2
0		9[47]	6		4[48]	8[49]		2[50]	1[51]		5
	4[52]	9		1[53]	2	2	5		1[54]	6[55]	
2[56]	0	2	0		4[57]	4		9[58]	5	0	0